MAN AS MICROCOSM IN TANTRIC HINDUISM

MAN AS MICROCOSM IN TANTRIC HINDUISM

Grace E. Cairns

MANOHAR
2005

First published 1992
Reprinted 2005

ISBN 81-7304-657-3

Published by
Ajay Kumar Jain *for*
Manohar Publishers & Distributors
4753/23 Ansari Road, Daryaganj
New Delhi 110 002

Printed at
Lordson Publishers Pvt. Ltd.
Delhi 110 007

Distributed in South Asia by
FOUNDATION BOOKS
4381/4, Ansari Road
Daryaganj, New Delhi 110 002
and its branches at Mumbai, Hyderabad,
Bangalore, Chennai, Kolkata

CONTENTS

ILLUSTRATIONS

INTRODUCTION

In western culture ideas of an identity between macrocosm and microcosm are as old as Biblical literature. In the Old Testament, it is said that man was originally made in the image of God but lost his divine attributes through sin. In the New Testament, Redemption came through Jesus the Christ who was both human and divine—as divine, being one of the three in the Trinity, which comprises the Father (God), the Son (Christ) and Another member, the Holy Spirit, which dwells within every man. Thus man may also be called partly divine through not identical with the macrocosmic reality. Yet Christian mystics from early Christian times have been close to affirming oneness with God, as heirs of the Neo-Platonic philosophy that stemmed from Plotinus and Scotus Erigena, his translator. Plotinus, himself, like the seers of the great Upaniṣads experienced an absolute identity between himself and the One, the macrocosmic divine reality. Professor Wayman in his article, "The Human Body as Microcosm"[1] shows how notions of macro-microcosmic identities were developed by outstanding western thinkers beginning with Plato, and continuing through such men as Jacob Boehme and other sixteenth century thinkers and how these were also developed in geometry and number symbolism.

Today scientific thought has become ascendant in the West. Does this mean that all ideas of macro-microcosmic symbolism must be abandoned? Our scientific knowledge, though still meagre at this point in man's youthful history, tells us that the matter of our bodies is the same as that found in the stars, our biological qualities similar to all other life forms, and our mental abilities akin to those of other higher animal forms. Yet our self-conscious awareness elevates us over other animals. In man, the cosmos has attained self-consciousness as it has also attained perhaps on other planets in this vast universe.This self-consciousness is called 'spirit' by many and likened to the Divine or God. The great mystics of East and West seem to have experienced a still higher form of consciousness, a superconscious state of oneness with the Ground, the Source of Being, the eternal spiritual Center that transcends yet is immanent in the concrete universe. In this state of oneness with the one, there is similarity, if not identity between macrocosm and microcosm. Man is seen not only as including all levels of the hierarchy of existence in the temporal world but transcending these in the superconscious state, the eternal immortal bliss.

Now, if there is such a spiritual reality, it should reveal itself also as unity in the natural world. In the realm of physics, Einstein sought a unification theory that would integrate the four basic forces of nature: the electro-magnetic, the weak force, the strong force and gravity. Experiments have been set up to investigate gravity waves,[2] which is a long step towards intergrating gravity into already existing unification theories that have successfully integrated the other three forces. Most recently, Stephen Hawkins, often called our contemporary Einstein, has made significant progress towards perfecting such a theory.[3] It seems the Grand Unification Theory will be realized before our century ends, and nature will be seen as one grand unity of which we are a part.

Along with this search for harmony and unity in the physical world, an outstanding thinker in biology Père Teilhard de Chardin, sees nature as a progressive evolutionary process from the world of matter to the biological and then the mind level which he calls the noosphere. Eventually the highest level will be reached, the ultra-hominisation of man into virtually a new species. The consciousness of this new being will include the entire cosmos and will have such complete control over the material and biological levels of being, that it will be able to break away from all temporal-spatial limitations and immortality will have been attained.

Along with progression towards this state, a new social order will also have been achieved because attainment of this new Divine state comes about through unity among men based upon mutual love. Père Teilhard points out that the great mystics have already attained this kind of egoless love for all that will become universal with the advent of the new species. God will be "all in everyone."[4]

Although Père Teilhard does not posit an identity between macrocosm and microcosm, he presumes that nature has been made in such a way that its processes lead to the divinity of man, so that he finally becomes an image of God.

In Indian thought, Sri Aurobindo has a similar view of man's evolutionary history and goal. He thinks of nature as a process of involution and evolution of the Divine, the Macrocosm, of Spirit. In its evolution, it rises from inconscient Matter to the biological level, Life, then to the mental stage, Mind, and ultimately reaches the highest kind of being, Spirit, the infinite Self. When this evolutionary goal is universally attained, every-one will have reached a state similar to the highest yogic experience, the level which Aurobindo calls the Gnostic, Supermind, the Superman or Supramental.

Spirit will now see itself both as one and many, because the Gnostic Being will know itself both as one and many, as center for concrete action and creativity of the Infinite Spirit. Since each human "Center" will know both the Infinite and all other centers with Gnostic knowledge-by-identity, there will be no overlapping or conflict in creative activities. Thus a new divine life will dawn in the world along with a new social order in which the good of each is the good of all, since each will realize completely his identity with all, a society similar to Père Teilhard's conception.[5]

Spiritually gifted individuals do not need to postpone this experience of Divinity until mankind universally attains it. Man already has the levels of Spirit within him along with the other three lower levels. In other words, *man is a microcosm* and his goal is to realize this. Aurobindo's macrocosmic evolutionary process of realization of the level of Spirit is paralleled in man in the process of the ascent of the cakras of kuṇḍalinī yoga. In this process, kuṇḍalinī (identified with the yogin) "passes from an involution in inconscience through a series of opening glories of her powers into the eternal superconscience of the spirit."[6]

Kuṇḍalinī yoga is the yoga par excellence of the Śakta and Śaiva schools of Hindu Tantrism, but their philosophy maintains, unlike Aurobindo's, an absorption of the yogin into the Brahman with no difference between the two, whereas Aurobindo does not think that the individual spirits are absorbed into the one, but are instead "poises of being" for the Divine creativity though with full conscious unity with It. Therefore in the former, there is not as much concern with social and political activity to attain a paradise in this world as in Aurobindo's thought. Nevertheless, great Hindu mystics such as Ramakrishna who, like the Śaiva and Śakta Tantrics, thought man should seek the ultimate goal of absolute oneness with the Divine, taught that service to man was a cardinal moral principle. This is because a philosophy based upon the identity between macrocosm and microcosm also affirms the identity of man with man as an essential corollary.

We have begun our study of the identity between macrocosm and microcosm in Tantric Hinduism with a brief background of how the idea evolved and developed in Hindu thought. We find its beginnings in the hymns of the Rig Veda, most obviously in the Puruṣa Sūkta (Rig Veda X.90) wherein the author derives the universe from the Puruṣa a gigantic Person sacrificed by the gods to form all the multiple forms of the universe. Yet the Puruṣa also has a transcendent aspect since only one-fourth of his being is the manifested universe; three-fourths of Him is the Immortal in Heaven.

The next stage of development is found in the Brāhmaṇas. The Śatapatha Brāhmaṇa's account of the Fire-Altar ritual shows that the Puruṣa of the Puruṣa Sūkta has now become the god, Prajāpati, ritually sacrificed to recreate the universe every year. The human sacrificer through performance of the ritual, becomes a microcosm through identification with Prajāpati, the macrocosm, the universe. Such identification wins the sacrificer immortality in Heaven. Other rituals in the Śatapatha Brāhmaṇa such as the Rājasuya and Vājapeya similarly identify the sacrificer as microcosm with the macrocosmic reality for the attainment of immortality in heaven.

A more profound approach to the nature of immortality was set forth by the sages of the great Upaniṣads. In this literature in the monistic Upaniṣads, the material and spiritual center of the universe is the One, the Brahman, who is the Source of the entire universe and one with man as microcosm.

Systematic formulations were given to this idea of identity in later philosophical systems such as the Advaita Vedānta and in the more popular Tantric systems. Since it is the latter that are richer in symbolism and therefore more influential in the arts, we have limited ourselves to them with only passing reference to other systems.

The outstanding feature of the Tantric systems is the use of yantra, mantra and kuṇḍalinī yoga to attain identity of the yogin with the One, the Macrocosm. Since the greatest yantra of Hinduism is the Śrī Yantra, we shall show how it portrays the entire macrocosm to demonstrate to the practitioner his identity as microcosm with It. Through meditation upon this symbol and by using yoga techniques, it is possible for the practitioner to realize his identity with the Ultimate Reality. The form of yoga used is kuṇḍalinī. During the processes of this discipline, all elements of the entire manifested universe, the macrocosm, are seen and experienced as residing in the microcosm, the individual, who absorbs the plurality of the many into the One, the eternal infinite Brahman, just as the One absorbs the multiplicity of Its created parts into Itself at the end of each cosmic cycle (*kalpa*). The yogin who has this experience sees all men and all nature as part of himself since all are phenomena of the One. Thus the aspirant attains complete reintegration with man and the cosmos and Liberation from the birth-death cycle, a common goal in most Indian philosophies.

Mantras, another basic aspect of Tantric systems, also play an important role in yoga, in most yantras and in Hinduism generally; but mantra in itself can portray the identity between macrocosm and microcosm and be a primal means to reintegration and Liberation when its goal is the experience of the adept's identity with the one. This is true of the Pañcadaśākṣarī mantra, a prime example in the Śakta system, and of the examples given of significant Vaiṣṇava mantras in our treatment of Tantric Vaiṣṇavism.

As we said, Tantric philosophies have been most influential in the arts of India. The Hindu temple is in plan a yantra that manifests the identity between macrocosm and microcosm as in the Fire-Altar built in the Agnicayana rite. In meditative cirumambulation of the temple, the pilgrim perceives it as a symbol in his own reintegration if he is aware of its meaning.

Certain sculptures, for example, the *Śiva Naṭarāja* and Vaiṣṇava sculptures treated in the text, also symbolize an identity between the macrocosm and the microcosm. These works, like the temple, are aids in the devotees' reintegration with the Ultimate Reality. Certain Hindu paintings have a similar function. We have chosen the *Dance of Kālī* and *Viṣṇu Maṇḍala* as among the more interesting.

To summarize, the basic function of such works of art, like the cosmic yantras and mantras is the portrayal of cosmic Reality in such a way that the aspirant sees the identity between it and the microcosm within himself. The Katha Upaniṣad expresses this identity in the oft-quoted passage:

> Whatever is here [i.e., in the microcosm] that is there [i.e., in the macrocosm].
> What is there, that again is here.[7]

As Woodroffe says, "The fundamental principle of the Tantra Shastra" is "that man is a microcosm. Whatever exists in the outer world exists in him."[8] Thus when in meditation the aspirant merges into the One, the Light Itself, he can say with Aurobindo:

> While there one can be wider than the world
> While there one is one's own infinity.[9]

NOTES

1. Alex Wayman, "The Human Body as Microcosm in India, Greek Cosmology, and Sixteenth Century Europe," *History of Religions*, Vol. No. 2, November 1982.
2. Dietrich E. Thomsen, "Trying to Rock with Gravity's Vibes," *Science News*, Vol. 126. No. 5, August 4, 1984, pp. 76-78.
3. Stephen W. Hawkins, *A Brief History of Time* (Toronto, New York, London, Sydney, Auckland: Bantam Books, 1988).
4. Père Teilhard de Chardin, *The Phenomenon of Man*, trans. Bernard Wall (London: Wm. Collins & Co., Ltd. and New York: Harper &Bros., 1959), p. 308.
5. Sri Aurobindo, *The Life Divine* (Pondicherry: Sri Aurobindo Ashram, 1955).
6. Sri Aurobindo, *The Problem of Rebirth* (Pondicherry: Sri Aurobindo Ashram, 1952), p. 76.
7. Katha Upaniṣad in Robert Ernest Hume, *Thirteen Principal Upanishads*, translated from the Sanskrit by Robert Ernest Hume, sec. ed. rev., (London: Oxford University Press, 1931, fourth impression, 1958), p. 355.
8. Sir John Woodroffe, *Śakti and Śakta* (Madras: Ganesh & Co. Private Ltd., 1958) p. 653.
9. From Sri Aurobindo's *Sāvitrī* quoted in S. Sharkaranarayan, *Sri Cakra*. sec. ed. (Pondicherry: Dipti Publications, Sri Aurobindo Ashram, 1973), pp. 121 f.

PART I

THE VEDIC BACKGROUND

I

ASPECTS OF MACRO-MICROCOSMIC SYMBOLISM IN THE HYMNS OF THE RIG-VEDA: MACRO-MICRO HOMOLOGISMS AND THE POWER OF SOUND

Macrocosm and microcosm in the Puruṣa Sūkta of the Rig Veda: The Puruṣa Sūkta (R.V.X.90) is where we find the view that becomes characteristic of many later philosophies and religious systems, the identity between the Ultimate Reality and the universe. The Sūkta declares, "Puruṣa alone is this entire world, both past and future; he is also the lord of immortality when he mounts above (to heaven) for food."[1] In this hymn all men, animals and plants, all of inorganic nature are part of, and one with the Puruṣa that is also "Lord of immortality." Yet only one-fourth of him is all creatures; "three-fourths of him are immortality in heaven."[2] The latter is his more spiritual aspect. In later symbolism this becomes a vivid realization of the identity of the noumenal and phenomenal aspects of microcosm and macrocosm, an experience which reintegrates the aspirant. Thus the groundwork was laid here for later more mature philosophical concepts that distinguish between noumenal and phenomenal, or eternal-temporal aspects of macrocosm and microcosm. Since the word puruṣa is male in the Sanskrit original, it was easier for the later Tantrics in their ideas and symbolism to formulate homologisms between the individual man as microcosm and the cosmos as macrocosm although this was not the intention of the original hymn. As Professor Brown comments, the connotation of puruṣa in its original content was not that of a male man-giant, but was a blend of the qualities of the gods Agni, Sūrya and Viṣṇu "treated as a rudimentary personification. . ."[3]

For the Tantrics who are Śaivas or Śaktas Ultimate Reality is neither male nor female. This idea finds its closest approximation in the Rig-Veda in the *tad ekam* (That One), neuter in gender, of hymn 10.129. This hymn, the first that manifests an explicit monism,[4] states that the entire universe evolved from a single neuter principle which it calls *tad ekam*. In the Puruṣa Sūkta, the gods alone seem to be excluded from the things and beings brought into existence at the sacrifice of the Puruṣa, but we are not told how the gods themselves came into being. In other hymns there are two original constituents of creation, the *Sat* and the *Asat*, but the composer of R.V.X. 129 abandoned this dualism. He thought there was neither Sat nor Asat before creation; creation evolved from That One (*tad ekam*) which developed from its own inner heart (*tapas*); then, once born Desire came upon It, the first "seed of mind." We have here a clear expression of the monistic concept developed further in the Upaniṣads upon which are based the monistic philosophies of Hinduism.

The magic power of sound (śabda) in the Rig-Veda. Sound as letters and mantra has been of major significance in Indian religion since Vedic times. In the Rig-Veda, another approach to the origin of the created universe is based upon the magic power of sound personified as the goddess, Vāc. The idea of the reactive power of sound is related to ritual. In the ritual performances, the correct words in the correct order, intonation and meter had to accompany the specific acts performed or they would not be effective. This notion led to the view of the creative power of sound. In *Rig-Veda* 10.71.1 and 10.82.3 when the gods name the things at the first sacrifice, these things come into being. It is this magical power of sound that is expressed in grander form in the glorification of Vāc in *R.V.* 1.164 attributed to Dīrghatamas, a vedic *ṛṣi*. In this hymn it is Vāc who is the One Real (neuter) rather than the Puruṣa of *R.V.* 10.90 or the *tad ekam* of 10.129.[5] We are told in hymn 1.164 that Vāc has a "thousand syllables," which means she "has at her command all possible sounds," Professor Brown explains, which she utilizes for the creation of the universe.[6] And like the puruṣa of X.10.90 only one-fourth of Vāc is manifested in creation; three-fourths is immortal in heaven, the region beyond the sun. Vāc is, thus, the One Real, the source of the entire creation.

In relation to the significance of *śabda* it is noteworthy that in this hymn, verse 42 asserts that the essence of Vāc is the *akṣāra* that flows from her, "on this the entire universe has its existence." This is again a clear affirmation of sound as the powerful creative symbol.

J.A.B. van Buitenen observes that "already in the Rig-Veda Saṁhitā akṣāra claims the position of a supreme principle, without, however, for a moment ceasing to mean 'syllable.' "[7]

The next stage in the development of the significance of *akṣāra* as such is identification with the syllable OM, but we shall discuss this later since it does not occur in the *Rig-Veda*. We should however mention the importance of *śabda* in the evolution of the idea of Brahman. This development also begins in the *Rig-Veda*. Professor van Buitenen quotes a verse which shows this: "As Jatavedas, most excellent Fire, sparkling in the syllable which is thy mother's womb, as thy father's father, seated in the womb of the true order, deliver the child-bearing brahman which radiates in heaven."[8] The interdependence, the interrelationship between Word and Fire is clearly brought out. The syllable (*akṣāra*), the smallest unit of speech, is the embryo of speech, and therefore the component of each word of the ritual utterance (brahman) of the sacrifice. Such a ritual utterance has a holy power of creating what it names. The power of the ritual utterance, the brahman, neuter in gender, later becomes the Ultimate Reality, the Brahman of the later Brāhmaṇas and of the Upaniṣads.

NOTES

1. Translated by W. Norman Brown in "The sources and Nature of *puruṣa* in the Puruṣa sūkta," *Journal of the American Oriental Society*, Vol. 51 (1931), pp. 108-118, p. 115.
2. *Ibid.*
3. *Ibid.*, p. 108.
4. W. Norman Brown, "The Theories of Creation in the Rig-Veda,"*Journal of the American Oriental Society*, Vol. 85, pp. 27f.
5. W. Norman Brown, "Agni, Sun, Sacrifice and Vāc : A Sacerdotal Ode by Dīrghatamas (Rig-Veda 1.164),"*Journal of the American Oriental Society*, Vol. 88, 1968, p. 199.
6. *Ibid.*, p. 217.
7. J. A. B. van Buitenen, "Akṣāra," *Journal of the American Oriental Society*, Vol. LXIX, pp. 176-187, p. 177.
8. *Ibid.*, p. 178.

II

MACRO-MICROCOSMIC SYMBOLISM IN THE ŚATAPATHA BRĀHMAṆA: THE AGNICAYANA, RĀJASŪYA AND VĀJAPEYA RITES

The Śatapatha Brāhmaṇa, which is one of the later Brāhmanas, is the most fruitful for delineating the further evolution of macro-microcosmic ideas. The sacrifices described therein most pertinent to our theme are the Agnicayana, the Rājasūya and Vājapeya. First we shall treat the Agnicayana (Fire-Altar) ritual which Professor Staal tells us is "likely to be the oldest surviving ritual of mankind."[1]

The Agnicayana (the Fire-Altar) Ritual

We may never know the original meaning and purpose of this ritual that originated in India about 1000 B.C.[2] Such ritual performances were common in India until 550 B.C. when the Vedic culture began to decline with the rise of Hinduism and Buddhism. Nevertheless, the Agnicayana was kept alive throughout the centuries and was most recently performed in 1975 by the Nambudiri brahmins of Kerala. The entire ritual was filmed and recorded under the direction of Professor J.F. Staal, whose magnificently illustrated two volumes *Agni* provide scholars with a complete account of what is known about this rite as well as complete day by day description and commentary on all aspects of the 1975 performance.

The Agnicayana is full of significance for subsequent religious and philosophical thought in India, largely because of later interpretations beginning with the Brāhmaṇas, particularly the Śatapatha (*ca*. 8th century B.C). The ideas of macro-microcosmic identity found in this work led to the *ātman-brahman* notion in the Upaniṣads, and the subsequent philosophical developments that we find in the thought of the Vedānta and also the Tantric schools. In this chapter, we shall see some major aspects of developments that begin in the Śatapatha Brāhmaṇa.

In the Fire-Altar we have a foreshadowing of the idea of the later Upaniṣadic philosophy of the identity of Brahman and ātman, though we must add that "identity" pertains only to the monistic Upaniṣads. In the Fire-Altar ritual, the sacrificer as microcosm identifies himself with Prajāpati-Agni, the Universe or macrocosm to obtain immortality. The Fire-Altar represents the Universe as Prajāpati-Agni, the primeval being who sacrifices himself as in the Puruṣa Sūkta of the Rig-Veda to become the created universe. The Fire-Altar ritual reconstitutes him.

The most important preliminary rite to the construction of the Fire-Altar in relation to the identification of the sacrificer (*yajamāna*) with Prajāpati-Agni is the sacrificer's carrying about of the sacred fire in the fire-pan (*ukhā*)for a time each day of the year that the Agnicayana is in construction.

The fire-pan itself is made of clay and the water used for making the clay is "boiled by means of resin of the palāsa tree"[3], because this tree is Soma, one of Agni's forms. Soma is also the drink of immortality, the ultimate aim of the sacrificer. In moulding the fire-pan out of clay, the bottom part is fashioned to represent the earth and spread out with the mantra, "May the Vasus, Aṅgiras-like, fashion thee by the Gāyatrī meter—for the bottom part is this (terrestrial) world, and this the Vasus fashioned by means of the Gāyatrī meter; and in like manner does this one now fashion it by means of the Gāyatrī meter."[4] [Note that throughout the *dīkṣā* (initiation ceremony) and the building of the Fire-Altar, śabda or akṣāra as mantra plays a large, essential and integral part. So we will not treat it separately as in the preceding chapter.]

Next, the air-world is fashioned as the lower side-part of the *ukhā* by means of the Triṣṭubh meter and the correct mantra ; then the sky is brought into being by means of the Jagatī meter and the right mantra; finally all space is included as the "four quarters" by means of the appropriate mantra, the one used by the All-gods to "put the quarters into these worlds."[5]

A further step to insure the sacrificer's identification with the macrocosm is related to the cosmic spatial aspects of Viṣṇu first mentioned in the Rig-Veda in the myth of the "three strides." The *ukhā* is made a span high and a span wide because Viṣṇu (here identical with

Agni), when an embryo was a span long, and the fire-pan is the womb to carry this divine embryo. (The three strides of Viṣṇu mentioned in the Rig-Veda are thought to include the universe : earth, air and sky—the "three worlds.") The sacrificer as part of the dīkṣā ritually takes the Viṣṇu strides to identify himself with the cosmic Viṣṇu who is also the immortal Agni-Prajāpati. By taking these three steps he gains the entire universe in miniature, the Macrocosm, for his steps encompass the earth and the air worlds also. As Macrocosm, he is Viṣṇu who is also Agni-Prajāpati. Passages such as the following show the assimilation of the sacrificer to the deity in the taking of the Viṣṇu strides: "Now he who is Viṣṇu is this sacrifice; and he who is this sacrifice is that same Agni in the *ukhā* (fire-pan): into the same (Agni) the gods changed themselves, and strode through these worlds; and in like manner the Sacrificer, having changed himself into that same (Agni), strides through these worlds."[6]

Another form of the Sacrificer's divine body is Agni as the Āhavanīya fire in the fire-pan, analogous to the Āhavanīya fire in the Fire-Altar that represents the awesome fire of the heaven-world at the macrocosmic level. This again manifests the main purpose of the ritual, the attainment of immortality.[7] Similar in significance is the wearing of a gold plate by the sacrificer,[8] which as the sun is inclusive of all space and time, for it has twenty-one knobs. As Eggeling explains, this means the twelve months of the year, five seasons, and the three worlds (twenty); the sun itself makes twenty-one.[9] This gold plate is worn over the navel (the Center, the axis of the macrocosm) of the sacrificer to develop his divine immortal body.[10]

In these ways the sacrificer is aided in his goal, attainment of immortality during the construction of the Fire-Altar. When completed, the embryonic Agni-Prajāpati (identified with the Sacrificer) is laid upon it and born as the child Agni.

Construction of the Fire-Altar: the First Layer. The form of the entire structure is a replica of the entire universe in its essential feature personified as Agni-Prajāpati. Its purpose, reconstruction or rebirth both of Prajāpati and the Sacrificer identified with him, make it one of the oldest yantra (maṇḍala) forms in ancient Indian civilization. The altar itself is constructed in the shape of a huge bird flying toward the East, the gate of heaven. The bird-shape is appropriate for enabling the Sacrificer to fly easily to heaven and become immortal when his full identification with Agni-Prajāpati is consummated through the ritual. The main body of the bird-shape is approximately in the form of a square about forty feet on each side. (It is interesting to note that the square, the form of the main body of the bird-shape, exemplifies the idea in Indian thought that the square, not the circle as in Greek thought, is the symbol of perfection.)[11]

The forty feet square is derived from the measurements of a man. Forty feet is four times the height of a man with his arms stretched upward; this gives the height of the square; the width is derived from the measurement from the tip of the middle finger of one hand to the tip of the middle finger of the other hand with the arms stretched out horizontally: this measurement is also multiplied by four to make the square of forty feet on each side. Not all Fire-Altars are alike, however, but may be of varying lengths the largest 101 feet on each side.[12] Professor Eggeling's simple diagram in its main features is reproduced in Diagram I.[13]

Before we discuss further the macro-microcosmic symbolism of the layers of the Fire-Altar, we should explain how the three fires of the sacrificial area also manifest such symbolism. The Gārhapatya fire (the regular householder's fire) is circular in shape and is the earth-world; the Dakṣināgni, crescent-shaped is the air-world; and the Āhavanīya fire, square in shape is, as we said above, the heavenly or sky-world. Thus the three fires represent the entire universe.[14]

The five layers of the Fire-Altar, like a typical cosmic *yantra* such as the Śrī Yantra, represent the hierarchy of planes of the macrocosm, in this case the Mahāpuruṣa, Agni-Prajāpati, with whom the sacrificer identifies himself. Before this first layer is built, the ground of the "body" is ploughed, watered and sown with seeds of a variety of herbs. Then a square mound is raised in the middle of the body, levelled off evenly to make a raised mound of the body area.

In the center of the raised square area, the priest places a lotus leaf with the words, "The waters' back thou art, the womb of Agni."[15] On this lotus leaf as the womb, he places the gold plate which the sacrificer has been wearing. This is the sun as we noted above. Then on the gold plate he lays a gold man identified as Prajāpati, Agni and the Sacrificer and represents the man in the sun's disk, divine and immortal. Next, an offering spoon is placed on either side of the gold man who lies on his back. These are the "arms" of Prajāpati. The sacrificer lies down on the gold man so as to rest his fore arms on the appropriate place; here the priest lays down the offering spoons. This act of the sacrificer again identifies him with the man-in-the-sun, Prajāpati.

On the gold man a naturally perforated brick is placed. (Another naturally perforated brick is placed in line with this first one which

PLAN OF FIRE-ALTAR

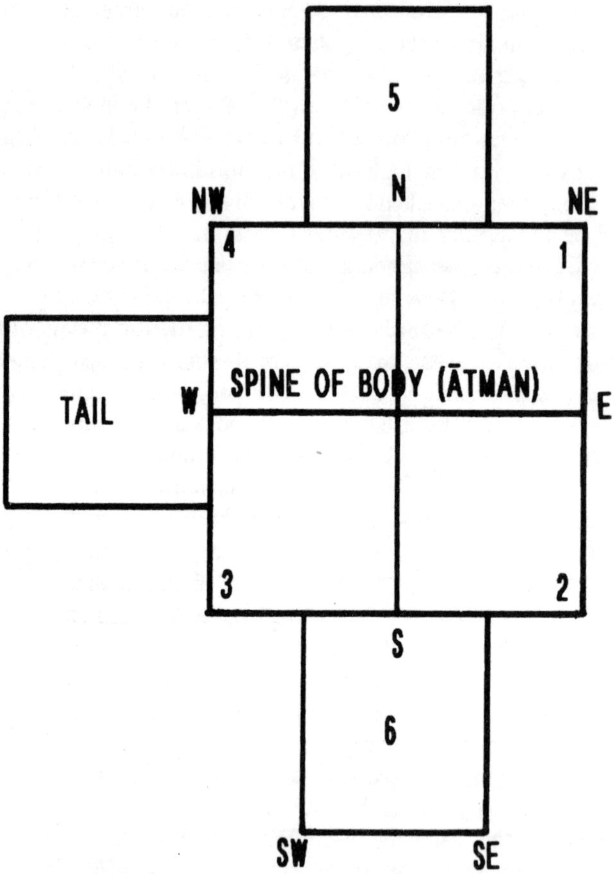

1. Left shoulder
2. Right shoulder
3. Right thigh
4. Left thigh
5. Left wing
6. Right wing

Diagram I. From Eggeling's Plan of the Fire-altar, p.419, SBE, Vol. XLI, Part III, *Śatapatha Brāhman*

symbolizes the earth-world in the third layer, the air-world, and still another in the fifth layer, the heaven-world.) Dūrvā grass is placed on the perforated brick as symbol of the vegetation of the earth since this brick represents the earth-world, and also food for the sacrificer.

Since all time is included in the five layers of the Altar, time in this layer is represented by two seasonal bricks. These signify the spring season.

In front of the perforated brick are placed several others, and finally the *asadhā* which represents the sacrificer's wife so that she can accompany him on his journey through the worlds to immortality.

Then, in a position facing the gold man, a live tortoise is placed representing the macrocosm: the lower shell being the earth, the upper the heaven-world and the space between, the air-world, still another way in which the sacrificer is identified with the entire cosmos.

At a distance of two bricks from the *aṣadhā* the priest places a wooden mortar and pestle. These are in the "middle" of the body and signify all kinds of food, breath and all trees, i.e. in general the plant-world. Thus by laying down the mortar and pestle, food, strength, breath and all the trees (this includes all vegetation) of the four quarters are included in the reconstitution of Agni-Prajāpati.

The animal world, too, is reconstituted, by putting the heads of five animal victims (symbolic of all animals) in the fire-pan, for by putting them in the "womb" they can never be diminished. The "vital airs" are restored to the animals by placing seven gold chips on each head.

The next important step is the restoration of the "vital airs" to the body of Agni-Prajāpati, which is accomplished by laying down ten *prāṇabṛta* bricks representing the orifices of the vital airs. These bricks link each of the ten vital airs individually to a *ṛṣi*, a part of the body, a meter and a season.

The cosmos is included in and also develops from the vital airs: all time as the Year, a complete revolution of Time included in the four seasons; all space and everything in it because the vital airs infuse the entire cosmic body of Agni-Prajāpati, and because by Speech, identified with Viśvakarman, all is done.[16] Thus the vital airs are of the utmost importance and have remained so to the present. The *Śatapatha Brāhmana* groups the ten vital airs in pairs of two, to become the same five breaths of later practices and literature.[17] It is by the vital airs that the embryonic Agni identified with the sacrificer is infused with life.

With the laying of the vital airs the first layer of the fire-Altar, i.e. the layer of the terrestrial world and of the developing embryonic Agni is completed.

Construction of the Fire-Altar: the Second Layer. The second layer reconstitutes that part of Prajāpati which is above the earth and below the atmosphere. Included again is a brick representing the sun and two seasonal bricks that signify the summer season. There are seasonal bricks in each layer because Prajāpati is the year by which is meant a complete revolution of time that symbolizes all time and space. All the quarters of space are again explicitly included making the time-space world complete. Bricks that signify all the earth's animals, including man, along with the bricks that are the vital airs to animate them, and *apasyas*, i.e. bricks that represent rain to nourish all, are arranged.

Construction of the Fire-Altar: the Third Layer. The Aśvins, physicians of the gods, who also bring treasures and avert sickness in the human world, were called upon to oversee the building of the second layer as Agni the first. In this third layer Vayu, the god of air and wind is regent; however, Indra, chief deity of this region and Agni also are called upon to help supervise its construction.

This layer reconstitutes the "middle" of Agni's body. The most significant brick is the second of the naturally perforated kind which enables the new immortal body of the sacrificer to ascend through the edifice to the heaven of immortality.

Again bricks are laid to represent space and time. There are also bricks representing all living things, especially the four-footed animals that provide food for the middle of Agni's body. In addition, bricks are laid down for the vital airs. A special *viśvajyoti* (all-light) brick represents Vayū, the regent. The other two bricks in the structure are for Agni in the first layer, and for Āditya (Sūrya, the Sun) in the fifth layer.[18]

Construction of the Fire-Altar: the Fourth Layer. This layer reconstitutes Agni-Prajāpati from above his waist or "middle" up to his head. Cosmically this region is above the air and below the heavens, and is called the Brāhmaṇ. Brāhmaṇ in the *Śatapatha Brāhmaṇa* does not have the same meaning as in the Upaniṣads and later literature. In *Ś.B*. VI.1.1.8 it is said that the puruṣa as Prajāpati "created first of all the Brahman (neuter), the triple science. . . hence they say, 'the Brahman (Veda) is the foundation of everything here.' " In *Ś.B*. VII. 3.1.42 we are told that the Fire-Altar is Prajāpati and "Prajāpati is the whole Brahman." These are the meanings of Brahman as the fourth layer of the Fire-Altar. As this fourth layer, the Brahman upholds heaven and earth.

To build up this fourth layer, *stoma* bricks are laid. These signify the *ṛṣis* (identified with the vital airs) and various other things such as Time in the parts of the Year; Space (seventeenfold as Prajāpati, but this, too, is the year), properties such as Speed, Vigor, Heat, Victorious Assault, the Womb, Strength, the Firmament—all again related to the year.

Then bricks are laid down for freedom from evil and death. Next, creation bricks are arranged to create the *varṇas* and all other living beings, all vegetation, the seven *ṛṣis*, the Fathers, the months and seasons. Now that all has been recreated, Prajāpati makes them "enter his own self," and the sacrificer does the same, a further identification of macrocosm and microcosm.

Reconstruction of the Fire-Altar: the Fifth Layer. This, the final layer, reconstitutes the head of Agni-Prajāpati. Cosmically it is the sky-world or heaven-world, the firmament, the world of the gods. It is a region "foeless, undisturbed," a heaven of peace.[19] To achieve the immortality necessary to abide here, has been the major purpose of the erection of the entire Fire-Altar from the yajamāna's point of view, as we know.

In the construction of this layer, the *chandasyas* (meters)bricks represent all three worlds (earth, the atmosphere or air-world and heaven-world) and include also a variety of other things such as space and time as usual. Then *stomabhaga* (praise-sharing) bricks are laid. All this reconstitutes the heavenly world. For the sacrificer, the thirtieth and last brick in the structure is the most significant, because it is the sacrificer himself and places him immediately in the heavenly world, his goal.

The third self-perforated brick symbolizing his goal, is the one from which he makes his ascent into the heavenly world. Next to it is the Vikarṇī brick as Vāyu, the vital air and further symbols such as two seasonal bricks for the dewey season to complete the year as total Time; bricks for total space and for the stars of the firmament—all this to make the totality of the macrocosm complete.

Related to the heavenly world of this layer, and its deifying of the sacrificer, is singing of hymn-tunes over the three naturally perforated bricks and the strewing of gold over this layer, Agni's now complete body. The hymns are sung to provide "sap" as the "means of subsistence," into these otherwise dry stones. The three tunes, one for each world (earth, air, heaven) have one grand finale "*svar-jyotis*" (heaven-light), since the sacrificer's goal is heaven. The chips of gold then strewn upon the Fire-Altar, Agni's body, bestows "immortality, that highest form" upon Agni and the sacrificer identified with him. As Eggeling observes, the priest in bestowing immortality upon Agni does this with the *double entente* of bestowing it upon the *yajamāna.*[20] Later on hymn-tunes are also sung to render Agni-Prajāpti's body immortal and likewise the body of the sacrificer.

The supreme significance of speech from the time of the Rig-Veda is brought out in the Fire-Altar ritual especially in the following passage : "These (hymns) are the immortal bricks; he lays them down last (highest) of all:—he thereby makes immortality the highest thing of all this (universe)."[21]

The Fire-Altar in its totality is thus all three worlds, all Time and Space and all that is therein, a microcosm that is the macrocosm; the sacrificer is the microcosm who, in constructing the macrocosm identifies himself with It thereby winning a godlike immortality in heaven.

Macro-microcosmic Symbolism in the Rājasūya Rite

As in the Fire-Altar ritual, he yajamāna, who is the king, becomes identified with the macrocosm. In the year-long initiation (*dīkṣitā*) ceremonies preceding the anointing ceremony (*abhiṣekha*) he becomes an embryo which, when born in the unction ritual signifies the rebirth of the king as the All, Prajāpati, the cosmos. The anointing ceremony, the central feature of the Rājasūya, has this as its theme. There are eight main episodes in this rite in which the king seeks to become the All, Prajāpati.

(1) Before the *ceremony* he mounts the quarters of space in four steps, but most significant is the fifth whereby he appropriates the whole universe because it reaches the upper region, the zenith which encompasses the whole.

(2) Before the ceremony a small gold plate is placed below his feet and one also on his head. This is to give his immortal life (see *Ś.B.* V. 4.1.12); it may also refer to an aspect of the king as the *axis mundi* as we shall see below.

(3) *The raising of the king's arms: the king as axis mundi.* In this episode the King is symbolically the *axis mundi.* (cosmic pillar), esoteric center of the universe, one with the All. The king's arms are raised with the words, "Thou art Mitra, thou art Varuṇa."[22] A verse is quoted just before this, which reads as follows in R.V. V. 62. 8: the rising of the sun, ye, O Mitra and Varuṇa, mount your golden-formed, iron-pil-

lared chariot; thence ye behold Aditi and Diti (the boundless space and the bounded)."[23] Heesterman in '*The Ancient Indian Royal Consecration*' observes that in this episode of the king's raising his arms "the notion of the *axis mundi* has a leading part."[24] Mitra and Varuṇa mount the chariot with the iron pillar or mount the pillar itself at the sun's rising.[25] The following story clarifies the symbolism.

Heesterman refers to and reiterates Jeannine Auboyer's interpretation of the significance of this stanza in relation to the arm-raising of the king. She relates it to the notion of the throne-pillar explicitly described in a much later work, the *Siṁhāsana* (*Thirty-two Throne Stories*) also known as the *Vikramacarita*.[26] The eighteenth century story declares that in the center of Udaya lake (also known as Lake Anavapta) there is a *yūpa* (pillar) of gold. From sunrise to noon, the pillar with the throne is gradually raised until it touches the disc of the sun ; then from noon until sunset it gradually sinks again into the lake. This cosmic pillar and throne are the sun's. The tale then relates how Vikramāditya as a *cakra vartin* seated himself upon the throne and accompanied the sun in its journey to the zenith, then descended with the sun into the subterranean world where the golden pillar rests on an altar of gold. Near it stands the goddess Prabhā (splendor), Mother of the World. From this subterranean region, Vikramāditya rose again on his throne with the sun and came to the surface of the lake at sunrise. This *yūpa* journey has varying time spans assigned it in the several versions of the tale, but in almost all, the throne and its occupant touch the solar disc.

In the Rājasūya, the meaning of the king with his arms upraised is probably identification of himself with the *axis mundi*. Before the arm-raising we saw that golden discs were placed at his feet and on his head. The golden disc at his feet could signify the Land of Gold as the foundation of the *axis mundi* according to a Buddhist 7th century account,[27] or the Altar of gold of the *Vikramacarita*; the golden disc on his head the extension of the axis to the zenith, the highest point reached by the sun in the *Vikramacarita* story. A similar view of the *axis mundi* is also found in early vedic literature in the Atharva Veda's Hymn to *Skambha* wherein the *skambha* ("prop, pillar, support") is the *axis mundi* or as Whitney phrases it the "framework of creation."[28] On this axis of the universe rests everything that exists in space and time.

(4) *The abhiṣekha (anointing ceremony)*. The king is baptized with seventeen kinds of water which symbolize the entire cosmos. (Seventeen is the number of Prajāpati.) This baptism signifies the king's rebirth as divine, the All.

(5) *The Viṣṇu strides*. Following the *abhiṣekha* the king takes the Viṣṇu strides which again give him identity with and lordship over the cosmos. Then he takes the chariot ride.

(6) *The chariot ride*. The chariot is the sun and its parts are the year. In the Rājasūya, the chariot ride in relation to the course of the sun functions to regenerate the world in the inauguration of a New Year.[29] The king turns the chariot so that it stands inside the *Vedi* (sacred area of the ritual) and yokes it with the words, "I yoke thee by the direction of Mitra and Varuṇa, the directors."[30] These deities are symbolically the king's arms and thus properly related to the rebirth of the king and the cosmos to bring in a new creation, a New Year.

The chariot ride again identifies the king with the macrocosm, the cosmos, as he ascends to the heavenly world. This is made clear when he descends from the chariot. His charioteer is not permitted to get down from the vehicle along with him; instead the charioteer is put up "along with the chariot, on the car-stand. Thence he leaps down: thus he does not descend on the same world on which the anointed has descended."[31] The circular movement of the ride is also significant. As Heestermann interprets it: "Moving round the world like the sun, the king renews it and at the same time reintegrates it into his person."[32]

We shall leave further discussion of the chariot ride for the following section on the Vājapeya ritual in which even more explicit cosmic symbolism is involved.

(7) *The enthronement of the king and the dice-throwing*. The throne-seat of the king raised high in the air is another symbol of the *axis mundi*, center of great power. Jeannine Auboyer throws much light on this in her book '*Le Trône et son Symbolisme dans l'Inde Ancienne*.' She points to the symbolism of the *vajrāsana* at Bodh Gaya as typical of the meaning of the throne in ancient India.[33] The throne, like the *vajrāsana* is the *axis mundi*, and to sit here is to become one with the universe, the All.

To symbolize further the throne as the *axis mundi* five dice are thrown into the king's hand with the words: "Dominant thou art: may these five regions of thine prosper!"[34] This means that the king is in the midst of and encompasses all space and time also, since the two are integrated in Vedic thought.

(8) *The dialogue between the king and the priest*. In the version of the *Śatapatha Brāhmaṇa*, the king has the might of the Brahman manifested in the powers of Savitṛ, Varuṇa, Indra and Rudra; but more than this, he is one with Prajāpati, the All and therefore his powers are unlimited. In the *Taittirīya Saṁhitā*, the king on his throne is the center

of a circle of priests and *ratnins* (persons whose occupations or lives connect them with important deities and who therefore receive oblations and are called "jewels" *ratninah* or *ratnins*). The priests are seated at the cardinal points. A dialogue similar to the one in the *Ś.B.* takes place, but the really significant thing is the position of the king as the center of a circle with the four chief priests at the cardinal points. The king is here the esoteric center of the cosmos whence radiates all being. He is again in this episode one with the All, the Macrocosm, Source of everything that has existence.

Macro-microcosmic Symbolism in the Vājapeya Rite

Throughout the Vājapeya ceremony the number seventeen, the number of Prajāpati, is pervasive because of its potency in identifying the sacrificer with the deity. Seventeen cups of Soma are drawn, seventeen animal victims are offered, seventeen drums are beaten during the chariot race, seventeen arrows are shot into the air before the race, seventeen competitors participate in the race, and there are seventeen rungs in the ladder climbed by the sacrificer and his wife, the *yūpa* (sacrificial post) itself being seventeen cubits high and wrapped in seventeen cloths.

Among the more interesting and significant rites are:

(1) The Pravargya rite. This is optional but significant for our theme. Eggeling thinks that the Mahāvīra pot used in this ritual "is the head of Viṣṇu, the sacrificial man, and sacrificer."[35] So in the ritual, the sacrificer's divine body is supplied with its head, just as the universe is supplied with the sun, its head (a golden plate is placed over the milk in the pot, a sun symbol). In this way the sacrificer becomes immortal (his divine body is completed with its head), but this is only one of the rites that offer the desired goal. As we said, it is an optional rite. Yet, the cosmic symbolism involved is very significant since the more ways in which one can ritually enact and thus ensure his immortality, the more certain it becomes.

(2) **The Brahman on the Cart-Wheel**. This is an essential rite. The cart-wheel is set up on a post as high as the navel (the average height of the sacrificial post). Either the Brahman mounts the wheel and turns it while he is upon it, or he turns it standing on the ground.

This episode is rich in macro-microcosmic symbolism. The wheel (*cakra*) represents the sun and the post the *axis mundi*. This is Heesterman's interpretation supported also by the work of other scholars. Heesterman comments: "In the pole surmounted by the wheel, may be recognized the *axis mundi* crowned by the sun, that rises out of the ocean and goes down with it."[36] In further support of this, Heesterman adds that the cart-wheel structure is placed on or near the *cātvāla*, a symbol of the ocean in the *Taittirīya Brāhmaṇa* 1.5.10.1.[37] If the *cāvāla* is a symbol of the ocean, this symbolism resembles what we found in the story from the *Vikramacarita* in J. Auboyer's interpretation described above in the section on the Rājasūya, the *yūpa* as cosmic axis surmounted by the wheel as the sun.

This interpretation becomes more important, when we come to know that the *yūpa* as cosmic axis surmounted by the wheel as the sun remains prominent in later times, most conspicuously in Buddhist thought and art. The most famous example is the Sarnath Pillar thought to have been built in the Deer Park at Sarnath to commemorate the Buddha's first preaching during king Aśoka's reign, but which may have been constructed much earlier. Only the lion capital of the Pillar remains intact in the Archaeological Museum at Sarnath, but we know from the account of the Chinese pilgrim, Hsüan Tsang, that the stone shaft was about seventy feet high and that the four lions on the capital facing the cardinal directions supported an enormous wheel signifying the Wheel of the Law (Dharmacakra). On the abacus of the surviving capital there are four animals and four wheels or discs, one facing each animal: a lion, an elephant, a bull and a horse.

Although more complex, the symbolism of this Pillar is essentially the same as that found in the *yūpa* with the cartwheel. In both, the shaft is the *axis mundi* and the wheel a sun symbol. Madanjeet Singh in his book '*Himalayan Art*' has a similar view. He thinks that Aśoka's Pillar and others of like pattern represent the Himalaya as world pillar and cosmic axis, and "in particular, it represents Mount Kailaśa near the sacred lake Manasarovara . . . 'most excellent lake of the mind' " and "epitomized in art as the lotus jar containing Amrita."[38]

Another relevant and entertaining legend of Buddhist tradition in this context, is referred to by Professors Rowland and Przyluski. As the latter reports, in the center of the earth in the Himalaya region is a lake named Anavatapta, the Lake Manasarovara of Madanjeet Singh. This lake is surrounded by four rocks each in the shape of an animal head, identical with those on the abacus of the Sarnath Pillar. On the eastern rock is a lion's head whence flows a stream clear in color; on the southern an ox-head whence flows a white stream, on the western a horse-head whence flows a green stream, and on the northern an elephant-head whence flows a yellow stream. Przyluski thinks that here we have the "four great streams of Indian geography: the Sīta, Ganges, Indus and Oxus,"[39] and points out that the symbolism of this legend is similar to that of the *Vikramacarita* tale. The Anavatapta lake and Lake Udaya are but "two names for the same mystical tank," for both are cosmic centers, the former the center of the earth, the latter the cosmic axis or center. He concludes, therefore, that the Sarnath pillar "is the image on a smaller scale" of the golden column of the *Vikramacarita* story which is why we find the four animals of the Anavatapta lake sculptured on it.[40]

Professor Rowland in his discussion of the meaning of the Sarnath Pillar and the four animals, shows how this symbolism has persisted up to modern times in a part of the ritual of the investiture of king Chulalongkorn of Siam in the nineteenth century.[41]

Before we leave the episode of the sacrificer on the cart-wheel, we should note that Professor Dumont in his article "The Indic God Ekapād," marshalls evidence to show that *Aja Ekapād* is a sun god and that his one leg is the cosmic pillar, the *axis mundi*.[42] Thus it seems fairly certain from all the data supplied by the above scholars that the sacrificer on the cart-wheel identifies himself with the *axis mundi*, the macrocosmic reality.

(3) **Ċhariot Race.** Another significant rite of the Vājapeya is the chariot race. As winner of the race, the sacrificer attains the goal of heaven; the goal post where the chariots turn is symbolic of the sun, door to heaven. The chariot itself is the chariot of the sun signified especially by the three divine horses hitched to it. In the 1950's, there was a modern authentic celebration of the Vājapeya in Poona, India. In the chariot race as part of the ritual, the priest recited stanzas which compare the charioteer's horses to those of the sun.[43]

After the race which the sacrificer always wins, he says, if a Brahman, "I have ascended unto the highest heaven of Bṛhaspati!"[44] If he is a king, he says, "I have ascended unto the highest heaven of Indra!"[45] In either case immortality is attained.

(4) **Ascent of the Yūpa**. This rite contains the most obvious symbolism of the *axis mundi*, the Mt. Meru or Mt. Kailāśa in the centre of the earth which reaches from the foundations of the universe up through the heavenly world. The *yūpa* simulates this *axis mundi* as the pole or post, the sacrificer and his wife climb to symbolically reach heaven and become immortal.

(5) **The Enthronement of the Sacrificer, as Prajāpati.** This rite reiterates the *axis mundi* theme. The throne seat is again an *axis mundi* of the same pattern as the Buddhist *vajrāsana*. In addition, the sacrificer is identified with the All, Prajāpati, center of the entire

cosmos radiating from the center of existence, the *axis mundi*, here the throne-seat.

In the above rites of the Vājapeya, as in those of the Rājasūya and Fire-Altar, the goal of the sacrificer is the attainment of immortality by ritually constructing a divine body that will be immortal and live in the heaven-world of the gods after death. Those who desire this, become one with the esoteric center of the universe, the *axis mundi*, the all whence radiates all time and space and its contents. Yet the aspirant, despite the rites, does not become one with the esoteric Center. He merely desires and believes he will attain an individual immortality in a heaven-world after death. We read in *Ś.B.* X. 4.3.10 that individuals who perform these rites attain immortal life after death, but those who have no knowledge of them or do not perform them, "become the food of him (Death) time after time."

In later macro-microcosmic symbolism of the more spiritual kind, as it developed in Indian thought beginning with the Upaniṣads, the microcosm attains immortality by becoming one with the All, the eternal spiritual reality, thus losing its individual identity. This is the affirmation of the monistic Upaniṣads upon which the philosophy of Advaita Vedānta is founded. This idea is foreshadowed in a late passage in the *Ś.B.*:

> Let him meditate on the Self, which is made up of intelligence, and endowed with a body of spirit, with a form of light, and with an etherial nature, which changes its shape at will, is swift as thought, of true resolve, and true purpose, which consists of all sweet odors and tastes, which holds sway over all the regions and pervades this whole universe, which is speechless and indifferent ; — even as a grain of rice, or of barley, or a grain of millet, or the smallest granule of millet, so is this golden Puruṣa in the heart; even as a smokeless light, it is greater than the sky, greater than the ether, greater than the earth, greater than all existing things;— that self of the spirit (breath) is my self; on passing away from hence I shall obtain that self. Verily, whosoever has this trust, for him there is no uncertainty."[46]

The significant advances that make this passage a bridge to Upaniṣadic thought are these ideas: that the Self is not a material body but spiritual and all-pervasive; and that this immortal self is realized by meditation, not by sacrificial rituals. It is this kind of thought centered upon the nature of the Self, individual and cosmic, and the relation between the two that is the dominant theme of the great Upaniṣads, where we find explicitly the revolutionary idea, the view that man is forever in his inmost and essential nature divine, one with the self of the universe.

NOTES

1. Frits Staal, AGNI : the Vedic Ritual of the Fire Altar, 2 vols. (Berkeley : The Asian Humanities Press, 1983), p. 1.
2. *Ibid.*
3. *Śatapatha Brāhmaṇa According to the Text of the Madhyandina School*, trans. Julius Eggeling, *Sacred Books of the East*, 50 vols., trans, by various Oriental scholars and ed. F. Max Muller (Oxford : 1879-1900), Vol. XLI, S.B. VI. 5. 1.1.
4. *Ibid.*, VI 5. 2. 3.
5. *Ibid.*, VI 5. 2. 6.
6. *Ibid.*, VI 7. 2. 11.
7. *Ibid.*, VI 7. 1. 1. , note 1.
8. *Ibid.*, VI 7. 1. 2.
9. *Ibid.*, n. 2.
10. *Ibid.*, VI. 7. 1. 8.
11. Stella Kramrisch, *The Hindu Temple*, 2 vols. (Calcutta: University of Calcutta, 1946), Vol. I, pp. 28 f.
12. *Ś.B.*, *op. cit.* Vol. XLIII, p. 1, n. 1.
13. Professor Eggeling's diagram in *Ś.B.*, Vol. XLI p. 419.
14. *Ś.B.*, VII. 1.2.12.
15. *Ibid.*, VII. 4.1.9.
16. *Ibid.*, Vol. XLIII, VIII. 1.2.9.
17. *Ibid.*, VIII. 1.3.6.
18. *Ibid.*, Vol. XLIII, p. 47. n.1.
19. *Ibid.*, VIII, 5.1.4.
20. *Ibid.*, p. 146. n.1.
21. *Ibid.*, *Ś.B.* IX. 1. 2. 43.
22. *Ibid.*, Vol. XLI, V. 4. 1. 16
23. Eggeling's translation of this verse from R.V.V. 62. 8 is quoted in *Ś.B.*. V. 4.1.15 from Vaj. S. X. 16. His translation is n. 1 to *Ś.B.* V.4.1.15 p. 93.
24. J.C. Heesterman, *The Ancient Indian Royal Consecration*: *The Rājasūya Described According to the Yajus Tests and Annotated.* ('S-Gravenhage; Mouton & Co., 1957), p. 101.
25. *Ibid.*
26. Edgerton, Franklin, *Vikrama's Adventures, or the Thirty-Two Tales of the Throne*, Harvard Oriental Series, 2 vols., (Cambridge: Harvard University Press, 1926), Vol. I, pp. 158 f. See also Jeannine Auboyer, *Le Trône et son Symbolisme Dans L' Inde Ancienne* (Paris : Presses Universitaire de France, 1949), pp. 58 ff. ; 78f.
27. *The Life of Hiuen-Tsianq* (or Hsüan Tsang) by the Shaman Hwui Li, trans, Samuel Beal, New ed., (reprinted: Westport, Conn., Hyperion Press, 1973; original ed. London : Kegan Paul, Trench, Trubner & co. Ltd., 1911), pp.

103f. See also Ananda K. Coomaraswamy, *Elements of Buddhist Iconography*, sec. ed. (New Delhi: Munshiram Manoharlal, 1972), pp. 52f.

28. *Atharva-Veda Saṁhitā*, trans., William Dwight Whitney, 2 vols. Hymn 7 "Mystic: on the Skambha or Frame of Creation."
29. Heesterman, *op. cit.*, p. 133.
30. *Ś.B.*, *op. cit.*, V. 4. 3. 5.
31. *Ibid.*, V. 4. 3. 23.
32. Heesterman, *op. cit.*, p. 136.
33. See note 32 above for references to the *vajrāsana*. In the 7th century account by Hsuan Tsang, the *vajrāsana* is the adamantine throne of the Buddha at Bodhgayā which is the *axis mundi*. This throne rose up when the world was brought into being at the dawn of the present aeon which, according to Buddhism is the Bhadra Kalpa. It is at the precise center of the universe and reaches downward to the "golden wheel." Coomaraswamy notes that this is the golden wheel mentioned by Vasubandhu in his *Abhidharmakośa*. Here it is said that at the dawn of creation the foam of the waters congealed to form the circle of the Land of Gold which Coomaraswamy thinks is the Golden Wheel of Hsüan-Tsang's account.
34. *Ś.B.*, *op. cit.*, V. 4.4.6; Eggeling's n.1 for the *Taitt. Br.* account.
35. *Ś.B.* Vol. XLIV, Introduction, p. xlviii.
36. Heesterman, *op. cit.*, p. 134
37. *Ibid.*, the *cātvāla* is a hole in the ground for constructing the *uttara-vedi* (higher-altar).
38. Madanjeet Singh, *Himalayan Art*, Unesco Art Books (New York: Macmillan, 1968; New York: Collier Books Ed., 1971), Collier Books ed. p. 15.
39. Professor Jean Przyluski's article, translated into English by Father Joseph Van Troy as "The Symbolism of the Sarnath Pillar," Appendix VII, pp. 8-92 in V.S. Agrawala, *Chakra-Dhvaja, the Wheel-Flag of India* (Varanasi, India : Prithivi Prakashan, 1964), p. 80.
40. *Ibid.*, p. 83.
41. Benjamin Rowland, *The Art and Architecture of India* (Baltimore : Penguin Books, reprinted 1958), pp. 41f.
42. P.E. Dumont, "The Vedic God Ekapad, the One-Legged Goat," Journal of the American Oriental Society, Vol. 53, 1933, p. 327.
43. "Vājapeya : English Commentary," a 13-page descriptive account of the entire ritual of the Vājapeya enacted in Poona, India in the 1950's which Professor J.A.B. van Buitenen recorded on sound film. A copy of this account was given to each student in class I attended under his professorship at the University of Chicago.
44. *Ś.B.*, *op. cit.* Vol. XLI, V. 1.5.4.
45. *Ibid.*, V. 1.5.5.
46. *Ibid.*, Vol. XLIII, Part IV, X. 6.3.2., p. 400.

III

MACRO-MICROCOSMIC IDENTITY IN THE UPANIṢADS: IDEAS AND SYMBOLS

Sages arose, around 600 B.C., who were not satisfied with the ritualistic approaches to man's nature and his immortality as portrayed in the Brāhmaṇa literature. Their discussions resulted in new views of the relation between macrocosm and microcosm. In one of the earliest Upaniṣads, the Chāndogya, we find the key saying, *tat tvam asi* (that thou art), a clear expression of the identity between macrocosm and microcosm as one spiritual reality. In this, as in the other great Upaniṣads, the method used by the individual in arriving at this conclusion is one of both reasoning and intuition rather than simple reliance upon traditional notions and ritual performances characteristic of the Brāhmaṇas. From the great Upaniṣads we have chosen the following four as most useful to our theme of macro-microcosmic identity.

The Chāndogya Upaniṣad

The seer of this great work, Uddālaka, must have had the overwhelming spiritual experience of oneness with the Divine Reality voiced in the famous words *tat tvam asi*. Perhaps his thinking about ultimate causes and processes in the universe led him towards this experience, or this mystical experience came first and then resulted in truth and significance through thought and reasoning; or the two processes may have occurred together, one reinforcing the other.

Uddālaka reveals his reasoning about his experience in the way he explains the nature of Ultimate Reality to his son, Svetaketu: "Just as by one piece of clay everything made of clay may be known". . . or by one nail-scissors everything made of iron may be known . . . the reality is just 'iron' "[1], so there is one substance, Being (*sat*) whereby everything that exists may be known. From Being, all is derived.

He explains to his son how Being entered the matter ("heat, water and food") of the universe as "this living soul (*ātman*)."[2] Thus man's inner invisible Self or Soul (*ātman*) is all-pervasive in the three divinities, also called the three forms, the red (heat), the white (water), and the black (food). These three forms are the materials of all things in the universe and anticipate the three guṇas of Sāṅkhya and other later philosophies. In 6.7.5. it is said that the mind consists of food, the breath of water and voice of heat. These are the body, but the body has its roots in Being, the *ātman*. In the *ātman* is the eternal and immortal essence of the individual as it is of the macrocosm. The individual reintegrates with this *ātman* by shedding the sheaths of the body (given differently in the *Taittirīya Upaniṣad*, see below). Then he becomes one with the One that is Reality (*satya*) that is *ātman* (soul) or spirit, and realizes eternally in full, the meaning of *tat tvam asi*.

Uddālaka also calls the Ultimate Reality the "one without a second." This identity of all in the One is brought out forcefully in the passage that uses the analogy of the single rivers that flow into the ocean. When they merge into the ocean, "they know not 'I am this one,' 'I am that one'—even so, my dear, all creatures here, though they have come forth from Being, know not 'we have come forth from Being.' "[3] The entire world has come forth from, is pervaded by, and returns to Being, the one Ātman, the "One without a second." The microcosm is thus one with the macrocosm.

The Bṛadāraṇyaka Upaniṣad

This, like the Chāndogya is famous for the teaching that the Ultimate Reality is "One without a second." In the Bṛhadāraṇyaka the sage Yājñavalkya in a philosophical dialogue with his wife, Maitreya, teaches her that the soul (*ātman*) is "infinite, limitless, just a mass of knowledge," not conscious and non-dual, not conscious because it is non-dual. He explains that where there is duality one can see, smell, hear, touch another, one can think and understand another; but when everything is one's own self, it is not possible. "Whereby would one understand him by whom one understands this All? Lo, whereby would one understand the understander?"[4]

This argument that the *ātman* the Self, is the Witness Self that, as such, can never be an object, was elaborated on by Śaṅkara and became a foundation-stone of Advaita Vedānta philosophy.

In another famous oft-quoted passage, Yājñavalkya discourses further on the nature of the *ātman*. Since it cannot be identified with any object or be called the pure Subject, because Subject for meaning has to be opposed to another, an object, and object has meaning only as opposed to subject; the *ātman* is neither; it is "not this, it is not that (*neti, neti*)."[5] Yajñāvalkya uses reason to demonstrate that the Ultimate Reality is indescribable. It is "one mass of knowledge" but without subject-object relationships. The non-dual one is All, the eternal, unchangeable, underlying Reality in the All, but is not the All as a plurality. One knows this truth because one *is* in his esential being this non-dual Reality ; and one can *know* it only intuitively by being It, by realizing his identity with It in a direct experience.

The Ultimate Reality is called Brahman in this and other Upaniṣads, as well as *ātman*. Yājñavalkya uses both terms as well as a third: *Antaryāmin*, Inner Controller. As the *antaryāmin*, the Ātman-Brahman is the "unseen Seer, the unheard Hearer, the unthought Thinker, the ununderstood Understander . . . other than He there is no understander. He is your Soul. . . the Immortal."[6] Also He is all-pervasive throughout the entire macrocosm. Western mystics, for example, Meister Eckhardt, have had similar experiences and views.

The Taittirīya Upaniṣad

In this work, the relationship between the One, the Ultimate Reality, and the world is conceived in the imagery of layers or sheaths, a view still held by modern schools of Indian thought such as Advaita Vedānta and the Śaiva and Śakta schools.

The Brahman (or *ātman*) is described as "set down in the secret place [of the heart]" like the *garbhagṛha* of the Hindu temple (see the chapter in part III on the Hindu temple). It is "in the highest heaven (*parame vyoman*)"[7] and is the real (*satya*), knowledge (*jñāna*) and the infinite (*ananta*).

We should note here in relation to our general theme, that this parallel and identity between the Brahman in the microcosmic individual (the Brahman in the heart) and the Brahman in the macrocosm (the

Brahman in the highest heaven) is the central concept in *yantra* symbolic diagrams of the cosmic type as, for example, in the Śrī Yantra treated in Part II below. (Mahāyāna Buddhist maṇḍalas have a similar meaning.) In these diagrams, triangles, circles and squares depicting "layers"or "sheaths" of the universe emanate from a center that signifies the Ultimate Reality.

The Taittirīya asserts that from the central reality, Brahman, first arose space (*ākāśa*) ; from space, air or wind (*vāyu*) ; from this arose fire; from fire water ; from water, the earth ; from earth herbs ; from herbs food ; from food, semen ; from semen the person (*puruṣa*).[7] The five elements of the concrete world in precisely this order of emanation, appear in many of the great Indian philosophies, notably Sāṅkhya, Vedānta and Vaiśeṣika. These "evolutes" can be reduced to the three of the Chāndogya Upaniṣad : air and fire belong to heat and the red color; water the white; earth, herbs and food to food, the black color.

Immediately after the enumeration of the five elements, the Taittirīya goes on to describe the sheaths of the macrocosm and microcosm. These are described in an ascending order in relation to the Return-to-the-Center, the reintegration of the aspirant. This is the return to the Utimate Source, to Brahman. First is the outermost sheath of "food," the gross body of both macrocosm and microcosm; then infusing this is the sheath of air (*prāṇa*) in macrocosm and microcosm which is said to be the life of all, of gods, men and beasts; it is the vital sheath.[8] Within this, is the sheath of mind (*manas*). This, in macrocosm and microcosm is the organ which synthesizes the materials from the sense organs. Within the sheath of *manas* is the sheath of intellect (*vijñāna*). This sheath is the "soul" of mind as mind is the "soul" of the sheath of air, which, in its turn, is the "soul" of the gross body.

Then within the sheath of Intellect, Bliss (*ānanda*) is realized. For the microcosmic individual, this is the Bliss of oneness with Brahman in his ultimate nature. The later Advaita Vedānta school of philosophy as formulated by Śaṅkara posits the sheath of bliss as another, the fifth sheath which also must be transcended to realize the Ultimate eternal Brahman without attributes (the *nirguṇa* Brahman of the *neti neti* passages of the Bṛhadāraṇyaka Upaniṣad).

The Māṇḍūkya Upaniṣad and the Syllable OṀ

OṀ probably meant Amen or assent and was used in this way in the Vedic rituals. In the Chāndogya Upaniṣad, OṀ is the "world-all," but the clearest expression of the macrocosm-microcosm parallel for this syllable is given in one of the later Upaniṣads, the Māṇḍūkya. This work opens with the statement that OṀ is "this whole world,"[9] and whatever transcends the threefold time (present, past and future) of this world, since OṀ symbolizes Brahman and everything is Brahman. Most significantly "this self (*ātman*) is Brahman," and this self has "four fourths" that are states of consciousness from the most gross to the most subtle.

The letter "A" of OṀ (in Sanskrit the letter "o" is a diphthong made up of "a" plus "u") is the waking state, the "common-to-all-men *vaiśvānara*)."[10] This is the first fourth of the *ātman* (and Brahman). It is the state of enjoyment of bodily pleasures, the "gross", by means of the bodily organs.

The second fourth is signified by the letter "U" and is the dream state (*taijasa*). The bodily organs are again operative, but they enjoy an idea-world, not the gross physical objects.

The third fourth is the deep-sleep state (*suṣupta*) wherein there is no activity of the bodily organs. It is called an unified "cognition-mass (*prajñāna-ghana*) consisting of bliss (*ānanda-maya*). . . whose mouth is thought (*cetas*) the Cognitional (*prajña*)."[11]

Beyond even this is the fourth, the highest state, the eternal, essential Self, One-without-a-second.[12] As in the Bṛhadāraṇyaka Upaniṣad, this state can only be described in negative terms, for all subject-object relations disappear.

Thus this Upaniṣad can give only a negative description as not a "cognition-mass," unseen, ungraspable, unthinkable.[13] It is a state called *caturtha* (fourth) in this Upaniṣad, but *turīya* which also means "fourth" in the Bṛhadāraṇyaka Upaniṣad is the name given this state in subsequent philosophical treatises.

The Śaiva-Śakta and Advaita Vedānta schools of Indian philosophy accept and build upon the basic ideas of the above Upaniṣads, namely : the *tat tvam asi* of the Chāndogya, the Witness Self of the Bṛhadāraṇyaka, the sheaths of the *ātman* of the Taittirīya and the meaning of OṀ of the Māṇḍūkya. Interesting correlations are made in the Advaita Vedānta and in the Tantric philosophies between the sheaths of the ātman of the Taittirīya and the four states of consciousness of the Māṇḍūkya to show the identity between macrocosm and microcosm.

We shall show how the Advaita Vedānta does this, since we treat the Tantric similar pattern of correlations in Part II below.

In Advaita Vedānta, the "A" of OṀ (A+U+M), the waking state of individual and cosmos, is equated with the sheath of food (*annamayakośa*) of the Taittirīya. This is the gross body of both the individual, the microcosm, and the macrocosm. The macrocosmic gross body is the aggregate of all the individual gross bodies, and as such, is personified as Vaiśvānara. The letter "U" of OṀ, the dream state of both individual and cosmos, is equated with the next three sheaths of the Taittirīya—the *prāñamayakośa*, the *manomayakośa* and the *vijñānamayakośa*, or sheaths of breath (life), mind and intellect. These combined make up the subtle body of both microcosm and macrocosm. At the macrocosmic level, it is personified as Hiraṇyagarbha or Sutrātmā. It is the "cosmic soul" and the "body" of the individual that transmigrates from life to life until released. In the dream state the gross body is inactive and the subtle body functions.

The letter "M" means the state of dreamless sleep, *suṣupta*. This is equated with the *ānandamayakośa* of the Taittirīya. At the macrocosmic level it is personified as *Īśvara*, the personal God who creates, preserves and destroys the universe. In the microcosm, the bliss of Īśvara is felt in dreamless sleep wherein all cares, all the distinctions of separateness and individuality are banished.

In recent Indian thought, the content of the five *kośas* is included in Aurobindo's evolutes (or involutes) of matter, life and mind. The goal of the evolutionary process, Spirit, is analogous to the ineffable Brahman beyond the *kośas*.

In Western thought, as has been said in the Introduction, Père Teilhard's evolutionary (or involutionary) process has a similar form : the realm of physico-chemistry (the matter-world), the biosphere (breath or life and lower mental functions), the noosphere (the world of human intellect) and ultimately the Omega Point, the Spirit of Aurobindo's thought and the goal of the evolutionary process, yet "outside all series,"[14] "pre-existent and transcendent."[15]

Gandhi, too, strongly influenced by Vedāntic ideas of the divine in man, called upon his adherents to follow the principle of *ahiṁsa* in setting up a new social order in India that would eventually give each individual the reverence due him as a ray of the divine light, as well as be an example for the emulation of the world.

The above short excursion into Vedāntic and modern similar ideas is merely to point out that the Upaniṣadic view that man is a microcosm, that he is in the deepest sense one with the Divine, is still a living and very fruitful philosophy.

We now return to ideas of macro-microcosmic identity in Tantric thought. We shall see, as the reader no doubt anticipates, that the Upaniṣadic idea that the Ātman is the Brahman is all-pervasive in Śaiva-Śakta Tantric philosophy and art.

NOTES

1. Robert Ernest Hume, Translator. *The Thirteen Principal Upanishads*, sec. ed., rev. (London: Oxford University Press, fourth impression, 1958), Chāndogya Upaniṣad, 6.1.4-6.
2. *Ibid.*, 6.3.2.
3. *Ibid.*, 6.10.1-3.
4. *Ibid.*, Hume, Bṛhadāraṇyaka Upaniṣad, 2.4.14.
5. *Ibid.*, 4.5.15.
6. *Ibid.*, 3.7.10.
7. *Ibid.*, Hume Taittirīya Upaniṣad, 2.1.
8. *Ibid.*
9. Māṇḍūkya Upanisad, 1.1.
10. *Ibid.*, 1.3.
11. *Ibid.*, 1.5.
12. *Ibid.*, 1.7.
13. *Ibid.*
14. Pére Teilhard de Chardin, *The Phenomenon of Man, op. cit.*, p. 270.
15. *Ibid.*, p. 308.

PART II

MAN AS MICROCOSM IN TANTRIC THOUGHT, RITUAL AND SYMBOLISM

IV

METAPHYSICS OF THE ŚAKTA AND NORTHERN ŚAIVA SCHOOLS OF TANTRIC THOUGHT

In the foregoing chapter we saw how the *tat tvam asi* concept, the central idea in macro-microcosmic symbolism reached the philosophical plane. The bridge between the Upaniṣads and the Tantric metaphysical concept involves the flowering of the cults of the great personal gods Viṣṇu and Śiva around 200 B.C.-200 A.D. Then began the formulation of the classical systems of philosophy; and about the same time, the rites, philosophy and other literature of what became the two major sects of Hinduism, the Śaivites and the Vaiṣṇavites, began to take form. This literature has come down to us in the Purāṇas and Tantras. Both of these literary forms manifest some aspects of macro-microcosmic symbolism, but the Tantras excel in showing forth all the aspects including art-forms. As Woodroffe comments, Hinduism has from medieval times to the present, been largely Tantric "and the main, where not the sole, source of some of the most fundamental concepts still prevalent as regards worship, images, initiation, yoga, the supremacy of Guru, and so forth."[1] The groundwork for comprehension of the macro-microcosmic symbolism we are to discuss in the following chapters lies in the metaphysics of the Tantra cults.

There are three major living Tantric cults, each centered around one of the great deities, Śiva, Śakti or Viṣṇu. Here we shall delineate briefly the metaphysics of the Śakta cult and in Part II, Chapter VIII treat the Tantric Vaiṣṇava metaphysical system. The metaphysics of the Northern Śaiva school is much the same as that of the Śaktas, so will not be dealt with separately. The literature of all these schools has a leading characteristic crucial in its significance for this essay: truth resides in the human body as microcosm and is therefore the "best medium through which truth is to be realized."[2]

In Western thought we find the same idea. We noted in our Introduction, that Wayman's article "The Human Body as Microcosm" shows how this idea was manifested in western thinkers from Plato to Jacob Boehme of the sixteenth century. We also noted a similar emphasis upon man as a microcosm in the more recent writings of Père Teilhard and Sri Aurobindo.

As we said, Śakta metaphysics is the same as the Northern Śaiva schools except that the Śaivas place primary emphasis upon Śiva, and the Śaktas upon the worship of Śakti. Śiva, the pure Consciousness aspect of the Ultimate Reality is, śava (a corpse); it is only with Śakti, the Power aspect of the Ultimate Being, that Śiva dynamically engages in the creative activity which gives rise to all the universes, sustains and then withdraws them in endless world-cycles. Śakti is thus the personification of this activity which gives rise to all universes. She is widely known as *Mahādevī* (the Great Goddess), or simply as Devī, and by many other names which are appropriate to the many aspects of Her nature, benign and fearsome.

In Tantric literature Śakti, personified as greatest of *devatās*, the goddess Tripurasundarī or Lalitā, is glorified as the Macrocosm, the Universe in its wonderful, fascinating totality represented symbolically by her primary form-symbol, the Śrī-Cakra and by her foremost sound-symbol or mantra, the Pañcadaśākṣarī Mantra. In the microcosm, the individual or *jīva*, she is *Kuṇḍalinī*. Each representation shows how the multiple universe issues from and is identical with Her. This enlightening knowledge is essential in leading the aspirant to liberation, as the self-realization experience of the identity of the devotee as microcosm with Devī, the macrocosm, who in turn is eternally in non-dual unity with Śiva (the pure Consciousness aspect of Ultimate Reality). All this involves an orderly metaphysical system of the manner of evolution of the One to the many, which in reverse order or involution points the way from the many to the One.

The One, the non-dual reality, is called *Paramaśiva*, also *Parāsaṁvit*, but unlike the non-dual Absolute of Advaita Vedānta philosophy, Paramaśiva is the coalescence of the "I" (*aham*) or subject, and the "This" (*Idam*), or object; or, in other words, of Śiva as pure Consciousness and the unmanifested Śakti. The "I" is the illuminating or knowing aspect (*prakāśa*) and the "This" is the known (*vimarśa*) aspect, yet the two are one, indistinguishable in their unity. The absolute experience has the immediacy of feeling and is best called *ānanda* (bliss). It has absolute unity, is formless, spaceless, timeless, all-pervading, all-knowing (omniscient) and all-powerful (omnipotent).[3]

From this One emanates the universe, the world of plurality, systematized in a pattern of thirty-six *tattvas* (principles). The general scheme of emanation as well as many of the *tattvas* are borrowed from the Sāṅkhya system of philosophy. Herewith is a descriptive list of the *tattvas*.

1. **The Śiva Tattva.** Paramaśiva has both a transcendent and an immanent aspect. The creative aspect is called Śiva *tattva*. In this state, Paramaśiva brings into operation the aspect of his Śakti which negates the experience of the perfect oneness of Śiva and Śakti and leaves the consciousness a pure "I" without consciousness of the unmanifested Śakti, the "idam." Thus it is a state called "the very void" because every kind of content or object (*idam*) is absent. The Śakti of Paramaśiva who in this way leads to the state of Śiva Tattva is the Śakti Tattva, the next evolute.

2. **The Śakti Tattva.** This is, as we said, the power of negation in the Śiva Tattva. When the Śakti Tattva blots out the perfect Śiva-Śakti wholeness and leaves only the experience of the subjective *aham,* the created universe begins to unfold from the Unmanifested, then through *māyā* to the manifested Śakti. The stages of this unfolding are represented in the following tattvas, a total of 36.

3. **The Sadākhya or Sadāśiva Tattva**. This is the first real emanation or creative manifestation of the new creative cycle. Although the emphasis is still on the "I" (*aham*) in the divine consciousness, the "this" (*idam*) is vaguely perceived. This tattva is the first stage in the evolution of the macrocosmic universe and the last stage in the involution of the microcosmic self. The goal of the latter is to attain oneness with Paramaśiva, and at this stage the "this" or world of objectivity is so dimly perceived that it soon disappears leaving only the *aham*, the pure subjectivity of the Śakti and Śiva tattvas which, in turn, merge into the Supreme, the non-dual Oneness of Paramaśiva. The reverse process takes place in evolution; thus the Sadaśiva tattva is the first step towards the world of objectivity and plurality.

This tattva is characterized by will or Force (*iccha*) as well as by Being. The *iccha* aspect of the Divine is present as the will to act, as Being or Force able to start action.

4. **Īśvara Tattva**. In this stage of emanation the "this" or *idam* is now clearly perceived by the subject, the "I" or *aham*. However, the "this" as the universe in idea-form is not seen as separate from the one Self, but as part of It.

5. **The Śuddhāvidyā or Sad-Vidyā Tattva.** This is the state in which the true relation between the I and This is realized. The *aham* and *idam* are equally recognized and separated in thought as different from each other; yet also as non-different and one because both are part of one Self.

This tattva is the last of the pure (*śuddha*) tattvas. They are called pure because they belong to the Universal order, and not to the world of limited experience. They are in the realm of truth, of things as they really are, in the region of the unitary experience of the One Self before *māyā* intervenes to give rise to the world of plurality, of limited beings who know only parts of the All and think of themselves as separate entities. The latter world is evolved in two groups, the *śuddhāśuddha* (pure-impure) and the *aśuddha* (impure) group. Within the *śuddhāśuddha* group are the following tattvas: Māyā, Kāla, Niyati, Rāga, Vidyā, Kalā and Puruṣa. The remaining tattvas all belong to the material world. These are: Prakṛti, Buddhi, Ahaṁkāra, Manas, Jñanendriyas, Karmen-driyas, Tanmātras, and Bhūtas. Each member of each group will be defined below:

6. **Māyā.** This is the obscuring power that the One throws forth to enable the world of *avidyā* (non-knowledge) or plurality to arise. Māyā brings with her a group known as the five *kañcukas* (*kañcuka* means "sheath" or "envelope") and the world of plurality, of limited beings, is born. At the same time, Paramaśiva in His transcendent state is unaffected by any of these obscuring forces. These five *kañcukas* are the next five in the series of tattvas.

7. **Kāla.** This is the experience of Time, of temporality. It is not empirical time, but gives rise to it.[4] It is the state of consciousness "contracted into the mode of temporal thinking."[5] Without the obscuration of māyā there would be Paramaśiva's experience of the total universe in idea-form in an eternal present.

8. **Niyati.** Apart from the clouding brought about by māyā, the unitary consciousness is characterized by omnipresence, all-pervasiveness. Māyā changes this to *niyati* (restriction). Experience is now subject to limitation in space, in field of operation, and so to sequences of cause and effect and similar limitation caused by lack of omnipresence in finite beings.

9. **Rāga.** This is attachment to one or more things, that is,limited interest versus the all-interest, the enjoyment of the All-this before the intervention of māyā.

10. **Vidyā.** This is the state of limited knowledge brought about by māyā, the opposite of the eternal divine state of omniscience.

11. **Kalā.** This is reduction of the omnipotence of the eternal state to one of limited creative power since the beings under the cloud of māyā are a multiplicity, a plurality and therefore finite in their powers.

12. **Puruṣa.** Under the cloud of māyā the Divine experience, as we said, becomes finitized; it suffers the limitations of the above five kañcukas. The experiencer in this state of limitation is called *puruṣa*. It is Spirit in its limited form.Then the obscuring force of māyā further shows its power by multiplying indefinitely the number of puruṣas, each believing itself a separate entity from the rest. At the same time, not only Paramaśiva but the śuddha tattvas (since they manifest the Divine unity) remain what they are. The world of temporality and mutual exclusiveness comes into being with the multiplicity, the differentiation and finitude of puruṣas. Puruṣa, however, belongs in the category of śuddhāśuddha tattvas since they are spiritual beings and an aspect of the one Divine reality. As such it is their goal, their destiny to throw off the obscuring veil of māyā, the world of multiplicity, and ultimately by involution through the five stages of the śuddha tattvas attain oneness with Paramaśiva, the non-dual One.

13. **Prakṛti.** This is the first of the aśuddha tattvas. It comes into being simultaneously with the appearance of the multiple puruṣas. The multiplicity of puruṣas necessarily involves relations between the puruṣa and an object; the object world is the world of prakṛti which is as multiple as the puruṣas.

At this stage of evolution, prior to the appearance of the next tattva, *buddhi*, the puruṣa is in a state like that of dreamless sleep; its feeling of being a subject is dim and indefinite; likewise the object-world is felt merely as a vague Something; this is prakṛti. Prakṛti in this stage is in a state of equipoise of its three components, the three *guṇas: sattva, rajas* and *tamas*,[6] and does not affect the experiencer. The sattva guṇa is the feeling of pleasure and peaceful awareness; the rajas the feeling of movement, of action; and the tamas the feeling of stupefaction, inertness and passivity. The bodies of all puruṣas and all other objects in the cosmos are composed of mixture of these three guṇas in varying proportions.

When the disturbance called *kṣobha* takes place in prakṛti to unbalance the equilibrium of the guṇas, evolution continues until the entire concrete cosmos is recreated. *Kṣobha* is caused by the Lord of the prakṛti Tattva[7] who initiates this disturbance to enable all the individual puruṣas to resume life in the *saṁsāra* in order to work out their merits and demerits (karma) on the way to Liberation. This goal is the reason for the recreation of the cosmos, just as the *pralaya* (withdrawal or involution of the cosmos) has for its purpose rest for the puruṣas, before they again resume life in the *saṁsāra*. The Lord of the Prakṛti Tattva has for his experience the prakṛtis of all the puruṣas as a collective whole. Prakṛtis is a plural because each puruṣa has its own prakṛti unlike the Sāṅkhya system of metaphysics. (Beginning here with puruṣa and prakṛti the following tattvas are much the same as in the Sāṅkhya system.)

14. **Buddhi.** With the disturbance of the prakṛti the next evolute, Buddhi, appears. Sattva guṇa is predominant here. The buddhi level of experience is one of Being only without consciousness of an "I" or of objects or sensations since these tattvas have not yet evolved. Next evolves the "I".

15. **Ahaṁkāra (I-Maker).** The "I" (*ahaṁkara*) appears. This is the "I" of self as the particular subject owning as "mine" the experiences of objects as well as the feeling reactions they cause. The universal Being-consciousness stage has been superceded by the particular-perceiving multiple consciousnesses of an endless number of personal egos.

The rajas guṇa is dominant in this tattva because in this evolute, Will, as the will to act, is its foremost aspect. Each particular puruṣa recognizes what he is capable of doing as a particular person.

16. **Manas.** This tattva is produced from ahaṁkāra. It has the function of gathering together into images the materials from the sense organs. The image is presented to the ahaṁkāra or ego which in turn assimilates it with past experiences through the operation of memory. Then the *buddhi* illuminates it by placing it in a more universal context.

Though manas is very active, the tamas guṇa dominates it because it lacks intelligence in itself. It is ahaṁkāra and above all buddhi that makes intelligent recognition of an object possible. Manas is also considered the seat of desire since it busily synthesizes into sense objects the materials affecting the individual puruṣa.

Buddhi, ahaṁkāra and manas, the mental factors of the puruṣa, together compose what is called the *antaḥkaraṇa.*

17-31. **Jñānendriyas (five senses), karmendriyas (five powers of action) and Tanmātras (five subtle elements).** The five senses are the usual ones: hearing, seeing, feeling, tasting, smelling. The *karmendriyas* are: speech, handling (using the hands for grasping, etc.), locomotion, evacuation (excretion, spitting, etc.), and reproduction (sexual activity).

The *tanmātras* are the subtle elements of the cosmos, also known as the subtle *bhūtas*. These are: the sound tanmātra, the touch tanmātra, the taste tanmātra, the odor tanmātra and the form or color tanmātra. They provide the "matter" for the transmigrating subtle body of the puruṣa. The next tattvas, the Five Bhūtas, arise from the tanmātras.

32-36. **The Five Bhūtas.** These are the material or gross elements of the universe. They provide the ahaṁkāra with its material body that completes it as an experiencing individual. These elements are ether (*akāśa*), air, water, earth and fire, the same as in ancient Greek philosophy.

Thus these all-inclusive thirty-six tattvas constitute the evolved universe recreated after each pralaya, identified with Śakti, the personification of the universe that emanates from the One.

This. like the Advaita Vedānta, is the metaphysics of an idealist philosophy, but also differs from the latter in its concept of the status of the projected universe. In Advaita Vedānta the universe, the world of plurality, has only phenomenal reality; reality itself, is non-dual and relationless. When the aspirant experiences his identity with the One which alone truly IS, he knows that the world of plurality and change is an illusory appearance.

The Śakta philosophy, on the other hand, posits the world of plurality as real, as a projection in space and time of the idea-universe that is eternally in the consciousness of the non-dual Ultimate Reality. Within It, Śiva (eternal consciousness) and Śakti (the universe in idea form) coalesce in a non-dual union. When each pralaya ends, another world cycle begins when Śakti goes forth under the obscuring veil of māyā to project (concretize) the idea—world of multiple puruṣas and their objects, that is, projects the universe of the thirty-six tattvas. In this way the concrete universe has real status, unlike the Advaita Vedānta system, though both are forms of idealism and both think of the Ultimate Reality as non-dual.

It is this metaphysical system of the Śakta and Northern Śaiva schools that plays a major part in the three cosmic types of symbolism in the Śakta philosophy: the mantra type, the yantra type and the symbolism of kuṇḍalinī yoga. Each of these symbolisms, shows the aspirant the parallelism between the macrocosm and himself as microcosm, the identity between the two and the way of return to the One, the *sādhaka's* goal. To attain this goal, he must comprehend the macro-microcosmic identity, not merely from the theoretical point of view, but from the actual experience of identity. We shall see how the three great symbolic forms of Śakta philosophy function as potent aids in inducing this experience.

NOTES

1. Arthur Avalon (Sir John Woodroffe), ed., *Principles of Tantra*, sec. ed. (Madras: Ganesh & Co. Pvt. Ltd., 1960), Preface by Arthur Avalon, p. 1.
2. Shashi Bhushan Dasgupta, An Introduction to Tantric Buddhism, sec. ed. (Calcutta: University of Calcutta, 1958), p. 3.
3. Sir John Woodroffe, *The Garland of Letters*, fourth ed. (Madras: Ganesh & Co., 1963), p. 85.
4. *Ibid.*, p. 141.
5. *Ibid.*, p. 142.
6. Jagdish Chandra Chatterji, *Kashmir Śaivism* (Srinagar : Research & Publication Department, 1962), p. 93.
7. Each *tattva* has its Lord.

V

THE COSMIC MANTRA : THE PAÑCADAŚĀKṢARĪ MANTRA

Background: Mantra Śastra in General

As we said in Chapter I of Part I, as early as Rig-Vedic times the all-important ritual performance was dependent for its effect largely upon the magic power of sound. Also we saw the creative power of sound glorified in the goddess Vāc (Speech) in the hymn addressed to her in the Rig-Veda. In this hymn we recall that Vāc was said to have a thousand syllables which means that she commands the total sound world from which she produces the universe. There is a similar view of the power of sound in Tantric literature. Sound is, in fact, so important that Tantrics call their literature Mantra-Śāstra rather than Tantra Śāstra.

In Mantra Śāstra the primary sound is called *para-nada*. This occurs in the first step towards the recreation of the universe. In this event, the experience in Paramaśiva in his ideal unity is negated when he brings into operation his Śakti as the power of negation resulting in a state of void. This "vision of void is accompanied by an indistinct sound called *para-nāda*, which fills the entire space."[1] One of the most recent of renowned authorities on the Tantra, Gopinath Kaviraj, asserts that *nāda* is "of the nature of light," and that sound and light are "phases of the same phenomenon" in the Tantras.[2] Woodroffe calls this phenomenon "stress."[3] This, which occurs in the Śiva tattva, and the next two evolutes, the Śakti and Sadāśiva tattvas, are the first expressions of the Supreme Will or Power (*iccha*) of Paramaśiva, the Absolute or Brahman, in Its movement towards the evolution of the universe.[4]

Next, at the Īśvara tattva stage of evolution, the diffuse light-sound is concentrated into a focus called *Mahā-bindu* whence emanate all the remaining tattvas that are the stuff of the universe. The Brhman's power of action (*kriyā-śakti*) is then brought into play and this supreme bindu (*mahā-bindu*) breaks into three : (1) Bindu—the lower (*apara*) bindu; (2) and (3) Bīja and Nāda—the lower (*apara*) nāda. In bindu Śiva is dominant, in Bīja, Śakti, and in Nāda, which is the product of the union of Śiva and Śakti, both are of equal strength.

The sound made when the *Mahā-bindu* splits into three is the Śabda-Brahmaṇ (literally sound-Brahman). The Praṇava "OM" is this sound of creation and all the wealth of symbolism it includes (delineated below). In man, the microcosm, it is in kuṇḍalinī. (See the section below on kuṇḍalinī yoga.) Also called Mahānāda, it is the causal state of Brahman.

The triangle of creative power—Bindu, Bīja and Nāda is the primary manifestation of Śakti Herself. As such, it is called the Kāmakalā triangle and is the abode of the Goddess as Tripurasundarī or Lalitā, for it is the Great Goddess Herself who evolves and becomes the very body of the universe. Before we delve into the rich symbolism of the Kāmakalā triangle, we shall mention aspects of it related to Mantra in general.

The Kāmakalā triangle as seed of the "endless mass of letters" and great Mantras is symbolized in the *A-Ka-Tha* triangle which includes all the letters of the Sanskrit alphabet. The sides of the triangle represent the following gods with their Śaktis : Brahmā, the creator deity with Vāmā : Viṣṇu, preserver of creation with Jyeṣṭha ; and Rudra, the destroyer with Raudrī. All these are aspects of Śakti as Īśvara of the Īśvara tattva. In relation to Mantra, the sixteen vowels beginning with *A* form the line Vāmā Brahmā; and the sixteen letters beginning with *Ka* form the line Viṣṇu-Jyeṣṭha; and the sixteen beginning with *Tha* the line Rudra-Raudrī. This makes only forty-eight letters; the remaining three of the Sanskrit alphabet *Ha*, *La* and *Kṣa* are in the corners of the triangle.

The letters are contained in the triangle in their subtle form called *mātṛkās* ("little mothers"). Their significance is brought out in *Principles of Tantra* which declares : "The string of fifty letters from A to Kṣa, which are the Mātṛkā, 'is eternal, unbeginning and unending, and Brahman itself,' "[5]

The mātṛkās belong to the subtle form of sound called Madhyamā Śabda. Its place in the sound world is to be understood in relation to the other three sound forms, Para-Śabda and Paśyantī Śabda and Vaikharī Śabda. Para-Śabda is Śabda-Brahman itself, a state of rest passing into movement.[6] It is the causal state of Brahman (the Mahā-bindu or Īśvara tattva), that aspect of the divine consciousness which is the immediate cause of creation; it is here that the dichotomy between the "I" or subject and the "This" or object begins. It is the cosmic dreamless sleep state of *suṣupti*.[7]

When the cosmic consciousness "awakens" from the causal state and "sees" (beholds in idea) the universe about to be created, the state is called *paśyantī śabda*. This is a state of general movement towards creation.[8]

In the next state, *mādhyamā śabda*, all the tattvas from Īśvara through Puruṣa are included. Although there is differentiation in the divine consciousness between subject and object, the objects are within the Self. This is the cosmic state of dreaming, *svapna*. Sound here is "special movement of subtle character heard by the subtle ear,"[9] the ear of a perfected yogin. The subtle forms of the letters of speech, the *mātṛkās*, belong to this stage of cosmic evolution.

Finally the Cosmic Mind projects the Idea—world onto the physical plane (*prakṛti* and the rest of the tattvas). Now there are material objects for the created *puruṣas*. The collectivity of these is the cosmic waking state, Jagrat. This is the stage of śabda called Vaikharī Śabda. Thought now expresses itself through the vocal organs of puruṣas as uttered speech heard by the gross ear, and we have the world of manifested śabda of Name (*nāma*) and Form (*rūpa*).

In relation to Mantra, the most significant aspect of this evolution of the Word , of Speech is the A-ka-tha triangle of Śakti which contains the mātṛkās, subtle forms of all the letters of the alphabet, and thus all the names of each and every object of the universe, therefore the entire cosmos.

As is typical of Tantric and much of Indian thought, the microcosm contains within itself all that is in the macrocosm. This includes the four states of śabda, each of which is described in relation to the cakras of kuṇḍalinī yoga. (See the chapter below for a full account of each cakra.) Paraśabda is motionless śabda in Kuṇḍalinī in the Mūlādhāra cakra near the anus. From this cakra to the Maṇipūra, near the navel, Paraśabda develops in general movements as Paśyantī. Then from Maṇipūra to Anāhata cakra, near the heart, particularized movement or Mādhyamā Śabda develops. From Anāhata the prāṇa ascends to the Viśuddha cakra at the throat and here we have audible sound or speech; this is Vaikharī Śabda, sound in its gross (*sthūla*) form.

The states of śabda from para (causal) to paśyantī and mādhyamā (subtle) probably refer to "causal stress" of the divine creative power, of Śakti, comparable perhaps to our concept of electrical energy, and not to audible sound until the state of vaikharī is reached. If we could read others' minds, we could "hear" or understand one another at the level of mādhyamā śabda or subtle "speech" for at this level the "sound" or energy vibrations would mean definite mental objects identical for all minds. Perfected yogins, it is believed, have this power of "hearing" at this level.

At the vaikharī level, the audible sound that would truly correspond with the mādhyamā form of sound would be the "natural name" of an object. The ordinary human ear is unable to hear these natural names. If one had such an ability, he could hear the sound of sap rising in trees or similar movements in nature, and these sounds would be the natural names; but only the Divine, the Supreme Being, can hear these vibrations and transmit such sounds, though imperfectly, to others, the perfected yogins. Only in this way can mankind receive approximate natural names.[10] The syllable OM, the "sound of creation" at the splitting of the Mahā-bindu into the triangle of creative power, the Kāmakalā triangle, is such an approximate natural name, Again, only the Supreme Ear can hear this wondrous sound in its purity.

OM, as the sound of creation is the *Mahā-Bīja* ("great seed-mantra"), Woodroffe informs us, because "it is the source of all others and of all compounded sounds,"[11] as it must be since, as we said, everything in the cosmos is included in the Sanskrit alphabet that encompasses the name-form universe; and OṀ immediately gives rise to the A-Ka-Tha or Kāmakalā triangle. Thus all other bīja-mantras, since derived from the mahā-bīja are particular sounds composed of the letters of the alphabet. The bīja-mantras of devas and devīs, like the mahā-bīja, OM, are also in the category of approximate natural names. Each devatā has his or her own bīja which is his *svarūpa* ("own-form").[12] The mantra is the devaṭā and the primary mantra in worship is the *mūlamantra* (root-mantra) of the deity. Strictly speaking, a bīja mantra has only one letter as the "seed from which the mantra springs,"[13] but at the popular level bījas often have two or more letters.

There are indeed mantras of great significance of more than one letter or syllable. Among the most famous and metaphysically significant in Śakta philosophy is the fifteen-syllabled Pañcadaśākṣari mantra, the mantra of the highest conceivable of all devatās, Śakti Herself as Tripurasundarī or Lalitā. In comprehension of, and meditation upon the Great Goddess with this mantra, the sādhaka may become one with Her and with Śiva with whom She is in eternal non-dual union, another classic example of macro-microcosmic symbolism in Indian thought and ritual.

Man as Microcosm in the Mahā-Mantra, the Pañcadaśākṣarī Mantra of Śakti as the Divine Mother, Tripurasundarī or Lalitā

As we said above, every devatā has mantra or sound symbol and also a form symbol, a yantra. In the following chapter we shall treat the form-symbol of śakti, the Śri Cakra, yet because there is an intimate relationship between the two, one cannot be treated without reference to the other. In the Mahā-Mantra, the mantra as sound symbol is central and the yantra of the Goddess is brought into relationship with it; in the Śrī Cakra, the form symbol, the opposite is the case.

First of all, it is of primary importance that the *sādhaka* (worshipper) knows the meaning of the Mahā-Mantra or of any other he uses or it will "bear no fruit."[14] Therefore the mantra must be fully understood. For an authentic account of the Mahā-Mantra's many metaphysical meanings in relation to man as microcosm, we shall rely upon Bhaskararāya's *Varivasyārahasya* (*Secret of Worship*). The author, who flourished between the last quarter of the seventeenth and second half of the eigteenth centuries A.D., is recognized as one of the greatest Śakta philosophers. Through elucidation of the complete meaning of the great mantra, he aims to show that through its use in worship, the *sādhaka*, the microcosm, becomes one with the Divine Mother, Śakti, who is also the Universe, the macrocosm, and through Her also becomes one with Śiva because the two are in eternal non-dual union which is the Brahman.

We shall not need to duplicate the complex details of the numerous meanings of the great mantra that signify this identity. For our purpose it will suffice to present the main aspects.

Bhaskararāya begins by identifying the Mantra with the Gāyatrī of the Rig-Veda.[15] As every student of Hinduism knows, the Gāyatrī is perhaps the most sacred of all mantras and is recited twice or thrice daily by all orthodox twice-born Hindus. According to Bhaskararāya, the Gāyatrī has two forms, one is the mantra of the Rig-Veda; the other is the esoteric one, the *Śri-Vidyā*, i.e., the Pañcadaśākṣarī in its total meaning.

To begin with the elucidation of this total meaning, we note that the mantra is divided into three groups. The first, named Vāgbhava-kūṭa, is composed of the letters Ka, E, Ī, La, Hrīṃ. The "Vāg" of Vāgbhava in uncombined form in Sanskrit is "Vāc" (or Vāk) which means "speech" and honors this ancient aspect of Śakti as Vāc in the

Rig-Veda; "bhava" of Vāgbhava means "existing, being, becoming," and in this context "kūṭa" means "heap, collection, or group."

The second group is called Kāmarāja-kūṭa and is composed of the letters Ha, Sa, Ka, Ha, La, Hrīṃ. The name Kāmarāja refers to Śakti as Kāma because of her creative, including procreative activity.

The third group, Śakti-kūṭa, is identical with the second minus the two Ha's. Thus the complete mantra is :

Ka, E, I, La, Hrīṃ; Ha, Sa, Ka, Ha, La, Hrīṃ; Sa, Ka, La, Hrīṃ. The Hrīṃ at the end of each group is called a Hṛllekha. Hrīṃ itself is composed of the following twelve letters: H: Vyoman; r: Agni; ī: Vāmālocana; ṃ: Bindu, Ardhacandra, Rodhinī, Nāda, Nādānta, Śakti, Vyāpika, Samanā and Unmanī. The last nine beginning with Bindu are collectively known as Nāda.

Directly related to man as microcosm, Bhāskararāya locates the letters of each of the kūṭas within definite cakra areas of the body. He places the first group in the area from the Mūlādhāra Cakra (near the anus) to the Anāhata (near the heart). The field of the second group extends from the Anāhata to the Ājñā Cakra (between the eyes), and that of the third group from here to the Sahasrāra (the Thousand-Petalled Lotus at the top of the head).[16]

Sir John Woodroffe agrees in general with the above, but differs about the number and location of the last nine members of the third group, the Śakti-kūṭa, beginning with Bindu and collectively called Nāda. Bhāskararāya arranges them in a hierarchical order with Bindu lowest in the middle of the forehead. Immediately above is the Ardhacandra shaped like the crescent moon; next is Rodhini triangular in shape with the brightness of moonlight; then comes Nāda resembling the ruby; Nādānta follows with the "sheen of lightning"; Śakti has the appearance of a nerve "rising out of the left of two juxtaposed Bindus"; Vyāpikā is next. The last two are Samanā with two Bindus one above the other with a line connecting them; finally comes Unmanī similar in form to Samanā minus the upper Bindu. Then above Unmanī is the Mahābindu.[17]

Woodroffe thinks there are only seven members in this group.[18] He locates Bindu in Īśvara-Tattva; Rodhinī (whom Woodroffe calls Bodhinī), Nāda, and Nādānta in Sadākhya-Tattva; and Unmanī in Śiva-Tattva. Woodroffe refers to Bhaskararāya's version, but thinks it due to a mistake, "Śakti and Vyāpika being regarded as distinct Śaktis instead of differing names for the third in this series of Śaktis."[19] Also, Woodroffe places Unmanī in Śiva-Tattva[20] which is above Īśvara-Tattva where he locates the Mahābindu. We accept Woodroffe's version.

In relation to macro-microcosmic symbolism, it is highly significant that these seven (or nine) Śaktis are the final stages in the ascent of the cakras of kuṇḍalinī yoga with its goal the dissolution of the individual personality and union with the non-dual Absolute. Here Unmanī in Śiva-Tattva represents Void, Śūnya, Nirvāṇa, a state immediately preceding the final goal.

Parallelism between macrocosm and microcosm in the five states of conciousness is the next aspect of macro-microcosmic identity presented by Bhaskararāya in his continuing elucidation of the Mahāmantra. In the Hṛllekha, Hrīṃ, the letter *r* is the Brightness which is the cause of the waking state (*jāgara*); the letter *i* is the Brightness which causes the dream state (*svapna*); Bindu is the subconscious state or state of deep sleep (*suṣupti*); Ardhacandra, Rodhinī and Nāda compose the fourth state (*turīya* or *turya*), a state of unity of consciousness; and finally the ultimate non-dual consciousness which is oneness with Paramaśiva called *turyātīta* is represented in the letters, thought of as *śūnyas* from Nādānta through Unmanī. Unmanī is "the sixth *śūnya* which is formless and is known as Mahā-Śūnya."[21] (The five śūnyas preceding Unmanī are named Repha, Bindu, Rodhinī, Nādānta and Vyāpikā.[22])

In his commentary on the *Lalitā-Sahasranāman* Bhaskararāya quotes Tantric texts which elucidate the significance of Devī's name as Unmanī, Unmanā or Manonmanī.[23] These passages which locate Unmanī just below the Sahasrāra, tell us that in this center there is neither time nor space, nor tattva, and there is complete freedom; that the object of meditation, process of meditation and meditator vanish; there neither subject nor object and the "ambrosia of freedom" is enjoyed.[24] This state fits in with Woodroffe's placement of Unmanī in the Śiva tattva.

The rest and greater part of Bhāskararāya's explication of the Great Mantra in his work on the subject is concerned with the topic he considers of most importance to mankind,, the goals (*arthas*) and the meaning of human life. Since there are as many goals as there are letters in the Mantra, he discusses fifteen. A few of the more significant in relation to the many aspects of macro-microcosmic identity are:

1. *A commentary on the meaning of the Gāyatrī.* Most significant here is his explication of the Hrīṃ of the Great Mantra. He says that it signifies the "Supreme Light." It is "the divinity dwelling in the heart, whose mark is consciousness."[25] Thus we have the identity between god as macrocosm (Śakti and Śiva) and the microcosm (God in the heart as the Supreme Light).

2. *Kaulikārtha*. This means the identity of the self, the Guru and Goddess. Bhāskararāya makes this clear by showing how the Mother includes all aspects of the universe. She is the three Śaktis of original creation—Icchā, Jñāna and Kriyā. She has the three guṇas, and the fire, moon and sun are her three eyes. This total of nine gives Her the "form of the nine planets."[26] She has the form of the twenty-seven asterisms (*nakṣatras*) since She assumes the form of twenty-seven of the thirty-six tattvas; the ten *indriyas*, "four" *antaḥkaraṇas* (there are only three : buddhi, *ahaṁkara* and *manas*), ten objects of senses, *prakṛti, puruṣa* and the *guṇa* tattvas.[27] (*Guṇa* is not a tattva for other authorities.) In addition, She has the form of the zodiacal signs. In all, She contains all aspects of the entire universe, all the thirty six tattvas.

Her "abode" the Śrī Cakra likewise includes the entire universe because it has its origin out of the Akṣāras of the Great Mantra.[28] The Bindu of the Śri Cakra originates from the three Ka's and the letter I; the other three regions of the Cakra from the Hrīṃs and the Hakāras (Ha's), the Ekāra E, Sakāras (Sa's), and Lakāras (La's). This shows the priority of Śabda in creation, a familiar idea in Tantric thought.

3. *Sarvarahasyārtha*. This is the secret meaning of the Great Mantra. It is the identity of the Great Goddess with Kulīnakuṇḍalinī Śakti as she sleeps in the Mūlādhāra, but when awakened by yoga of the sādhaka ascends through the cakras of the body to the Sahasrāra where there is non-dual union of Śiva and Śakti. It is with the latter that the yogin-aspirant identifies himself and thus attains *mokṣa*. It is the identity of the self of the sādhaka with Kuṇḍalinī that is the esoteric meaning of the Śrīvidyā or Mahāmantra.

4. *Mahātattvārtha*. This is the ultimate meaning of the Great Mantra. It is that the transcendent Goddess in non-dual union with Śiva is the One, Brahman, and not merely identical with the universe. This Brahman is Consciousness and Bliss, and transcends the thirty-six tattvas, is "bigger than the biggest and smaller than the smallest."[29] It is not comprehensible by the mind or the sense organs, but only by becoming one with It.

5. *Mahāvākyārtha*. This concerns the meaning of the great utterances or suggestive sentences implied by the letters of the Vidyā. This overall meaning is another affirmation of the identity of the Jīva and the Brahman.[30]

To summarize, the Great Mantra in its many meanings has as its general purport the affirmation of the identity of the individual soul with the universal soul, Brahman, as the non-dual unity of Śiva and Śakti. The many homologisms, likenesses between macrocosm and microcosm. expressed in Bhāskararāya's work are potent aids in reintegration of the yogin whose final goal is actual experience of this oneness with the Ultimate Reality. Bhāskararāya affirms that Śiva, Śakti, the Guru and the *sādhaka* at the highest level of spiritual realization are One in the non-dual unity which is Brahman. At the end of his work Bhāskararāya offers a reverent tribute to his own guru, whom he pictures seated on the A, Ka, Tha triangle (the Kāmakalā triangle). This triangle is the center of the celebrated Śrī Cakra, subject of the following chapter.

NOTES

1. Gopinath Kaviraj, *Aspects of Indian Thought* (Burdwan: The University of Burdwan, 1966), p. 194.
2. *Ibid.*
3. Woodroffe, *Garland of Letters, op. cit.*, chap. V. "Śakti as Stress."
4. Kaviraj, *op. cit.*, p. 194.
5. *Principles of Tantra* : The Tantratattva of Śrīyukta Śiva Candra Vidyārṇava Bhattacārya Mahodaya, Introductions Arthur Avalon and Śrīyukta Baradā Kantā Majumdār, ed. Arthur Avalon (Madras: Ganesh & Co. , 1960), p. 521.
6. Woodroffe, *Garland of Letters, op. cit.*, p. 232.
7. Arthur Avalon, *Śakti and Śakta* (Madras: Ganesh & Co., 1959), p. 497 f.
8. Woodroffe, *Garland of Letters, op. cit.*, p. 232.
9. *Ibid.*, p. 232.
10. *Ibid.*, p. 65.
11. *Ibid.*, p. 232.
12. *Ibid.*, p. 234.
13. *Ibid.*
14. Śrī Bhāskararāya Makhin, *Varivasya-Rahasya and Its Commentary*, ed. with English trans. by Pandit S. Subrahmanya Sastri. 3d ed. (Madras : The Adyar Library and Research Centre, 1968), v. 54, p. 35.
15. *Ibid.*, vv. 60-63, pp. 39-41.
16. *Ibid.*, vv. 20, 21, p. 16.
17. *Ibid.*, vv. 22-26 p. 20.
18. Avalon, Arthur, trans. *The Serpent Power*, 6th ed. (Madras: Ganesh & Co., 1958), p. 143.
19. *Ibid.*, also see p. 425.
20. Woodroffe, *Garland of Letters. op. cit.*, p. 86.
21. *Ibid.*, v. 42, p. 29.
22. *Ibid.*
23. *Lalitā-Sahasranāman* with Bhāskararāya's Commentary, trans, R. Ananthakrishna Sastry, 2d ed. (Madras: The Theosophical Publishing House, 1951, reprinted 1970), p. 121.
24. *Ibid.*

25. Here and throughout his discussion of this mantra, Bhāskararāya refers to the meaning of the Gāyatrī as set forth in the *Tripurātāpinī Upaniṣad*, although he writes in the *Varivasyā-Rahasya*, v. 63. p. 41. that he is referring to the *Tripurā Upaniṣad*, a different Śakta Upaniṣad. See *Śakta Upaniṣads*, trans. A.G. Krishna Warrier (Madras: Adyar Library and Research Centre, 1967), *Tripurātapinī Upaniṣad*, pp. 1-8 for this Upaniṣads's commentary on the Gāyatrī. For the original Sanskrit version of both Upaniṣads see *The Śakta Upaniṣads with the Commentary of Śri Upaniṣad-Brahmā-Yogin*, ed. Pandit A. Mahadeva Sastri (Madras : The Adyar Library, 1950) for both the Sanskrit texts.
26. Bhāskararāya. *Varivasya-Rahasyā, op.cit.*, v. 84, p. 76.
27. *Ibid.*, v. 85, p. 77.
28. *Ibid.*, vv. 99, 100, p. 88.
29. *Ibid.*, v. 108. p. 93.
30. *Ibid.*, vv. 141, 142, p. 112.

VI

THE ŚRI YANTRA (OR CAKRA)

As the Pañcadaśākṣarī Mantra is Devī's essential sound-body, the Śrī Yantra best represents her form-body, the universe. The *Kāmakalā Vilāsa* says: "The wise know no difference between the Maheśī and the Cakra."[1] The Goddess is the subtle form of both, and neither is there any difference between the two in the gross form.[2]

As the essential form of the Great Goddess, the Śrī Yantra is still much revered, not only by Tantrics, but by adherents of India's most intellectual philosophical school, the Advaita Vedānta. In 1978 it was mentioned in literature sent out to scholars of Indian thought, describing the celebration in Kalādi, Śaṅkara's birthplace, of the inauguration of Ādi Śaṅkara Bhagavat Pāda's Kīrti Stambha of nine stories. The four-page flier announcing the event included a short summary of Śaṅkara's life and achievements. Included among the latter was the installation of the Śrī Cakra. Moreover, there is a Śrī Cakra in each of the "maths" still thriving today that were established by Śaṅkara himself.

The Śrī Cakra is Hinduism's best-known yantra. It has the characteristic function of the cosmic maṇḍala, realization by the devotee of the identity between himself and the cosmos. The cosmos is, itself, the body of the Devī projected and withdrawn throughout the endless world cycles. The Śrī represents this aspect of the cosmos as well as the spiritual, subtle aspects of the Great Goddess who, as deity of this Cakra, is called Lalitā or Tripurasundarī.

In the Lalitā-Sahāsranāman, the Śrī Cakra is called an abode of Lalitā. Another of her thousand names is "Ruler of the beautiful city."[3] As described in a Tantric work, this city is "outside and beyond the countless myriads of world systems, in the centre of the ocean of nectar, more than a thousand crores in extent . . . and adorned with twenty-five walls representing the twenty-five tattvas."[4] In another Tantric work, Bhāskararāya adds, the Beautiful City is interpreted as the Śrī Cakra.[5]

Further information about Devī's abode is given by Bhāskararāya, under Lalitā's name Pañcabrahmāsansathitā (Sitting-upon-a-seat-formed-by-five-Brahmās). In this context, he quotes Tantric treatises that portray Lalitā's "supreme abode" as built of cintamāṇi stone and containing a glorious couch upon which Lalitā lies. The couch is Śiva, himself, the pillow Īśana (a form of Śiva), the mat is Sadāśiva (another form of Śiva), Hari (a name of Viṣṇu), a Rudra and Īśāna (who also seems to be her pillow). Having these great deities as her pillow means that they cannot act without the power or energy which is Devī.[6]

The *cintamāṇi* place is located in the midst of an immense lotus forest. Bhāskararāya comments that the thousand-petalled lotus in the Sahāsrāra Cakra of the individual "is also called Padmāṭavī (lotus-forest). This, he says, shows the identity between Lalitā, the macrocosm, and the individual, the microcosm,[7] the dominant theme of the entire cakra system. Professor W. Norman Brown in his Introduction to this translation of the *Saundaryalaharī* locates the Śrī Cakra's "mystic diagram" at the top of Devī's head in the *sahasrāra*, or thousand-petalled lotus.[8] In this work, the entire cosmos is conceived as the body of Mahādevī with the six cakras of kuṇḍalinī yoga located in Her body as the macrocosmic universe; but the identity of these macrocosmic cakras with those of the individual, the microcosm, is not mentioned. Professor Brown thinks that this identification was made later than 1000 A.D in the late yoga or Śaiva Upaniṣads.[9]

The central feature of the Śrī Cakra is the series of symbolic interlocking triangles in the center. These are surrounded by two circles of lotus petals bordered by three circular lines. Outside these is a square with four gateways,, one at each of the cardinal points. The interlocking triangles are composed of five inverted triangles, the Śakti triangles, and four upright triangles, the Śiva triangles. The center triangle formed by interlocking Śakti triangles, called the Kāmakalā Triangle, is the core of the diagram whence the entire universe symbolized by the Śrī Cakra emanates. In its center is the Mahābindu, the Sarvānandamaya Cakra. This is the first, beginning from the center, of the total of nine cakras of this Yantra. Its function is in its use by the aspirant for enlightenment in his spiritual journey towards mokṣa. The Cakra clearly delineates the identity between the form-body of the Great Goddess and that of the devotee in all aspects, material, vital, mental and spiritual. We shall follow the aspirant's journey through the nine cakras to see how

THE ŚRĪ YANTRA

Diagram II.

each manifests significant aspects of this identity "beginning with the outermost."

The Bhupūra or Trailokyamohana Cakra. This is the ninth, the outermost cakra symbolized by a square formed by a border of three lines. Here, there are ten Siddhis of the macrocosm who are related to the power, emotions or sentiments of the individual, the microcosm. In the middle line of this cakra, are eight Mātṛkās that represent distorted forms of emotion with resulting sin and merit. Also they symbolize the substances of the body in macrocosm and microcosm, the seven *dhātus* (bone, fat, flesh, blood, skin, marrow and semen—the same in both microcosm and macrocosm); the eighth is Devī's own form.

In the innermost line are ten Mudrā Śaktis, one for each of the nine cakras, the tenth above and transcending all. They are characterized by a transcendent divine consciousness (*cidghana*) and are glorious powers resembling the morning sun in their brilliance. They are also transformations of the Śaktis of the Nine Nāthas, the nine apertures of the body of both macrocosm and microcosm, i.e., of the sādhaka's body, the microcosm here. These apertures are the two eyes, the mouth, the two ears, the reproductive organ and the anus. A well-known Śakta Upaniṣad, the *Bhāvanopaniṣad*, considered *śruti* by the Śaktas, says:

> Of that Power the body with its nine orifices is the form.
> It is the holy Wheel in the guise of the nine wheels.[10]

Bhāskararāya in his commentary on this passage explains, that the "Power" is Parāśakti (Tripurasundarī, or the Great Goddess) and the Holy Wheel the Śrī Cakra. There are many other homologisms in this Upaniṣad to show how the Śrī Cakra, because it represents both macrocosm and microcosm is an aid to the devotee in his quest for self-realization, i.e, "the identity of the three: knowledge, its object and the knower." Third is the "worship rendered to the holy Wheel."[11] The nine Nathas appear again in the first cakra, the Sarvānandamaya.

Sarvāśāparipuraka ("Fulfiller of all Hopes"), the eighth cakra. This is the sixteen-petalled lotus which the aspirant enters next in his contemplation. Here are the five *bhūtas* (material elements), the ten senses (five of perception and five of action), *manas*, *ahaṁkāra* and *buddhi*. In addition, the deities here represent control over the *bhūtas* and all other tattvas. The *sādhaka* not only identifies himself with these aspects of the macrocosm, but disciplines himself in control over them in himself and others.[12]

Sarvasaṁkṣobhaṇa ("All-moving") the seventh cakra. This is the lotus of eight petals outside the sixth cakra. Here the aspirant identifies himself again with *tattvas* of both macrocosm and himself as microcosm. These are Prakṛti, Buddhi, Ahaṁkara and the five Tanmātras all represented as the womanly forms of yoginīs.

Śabda, too, plays a significant part in this cakra with the appearance of Vaikharī-Vāk. *Śabda* in its Vaikharī (gross uttered) form is creator of the concrete universe "composed of the collectivity of the letters" of the alphabet.[13] The power of sound, we know, brings forth the gross material world of physical bodies, here it refers to the all-embracing physical body, the body of the Great Goddess which is the cosmos. Thus this and the eight and ninth cakras are the gross or physical sheath of macrocosm and microcosm. With the sixth cakra we begin to treat the subtle body and vital sheath of both.[14]

Sarvasaubhāgyadāyaka ("Giver of all Prosperity"), the sixth cakra. With this cakra the yogin begins his identification with the subtle body of the Great Goddess. This is the cakra of fourteen triangles outside the outer cakra of ten triangles. Here he finds the fourteen vowels of the Sanskrit alphabet. In this and the two preceding, the fifth and fourth cakras, we have the total of fifty-one letters of this alphabet all in their unuttered form and therefore belonging to Madhymā Vāk which symbolized the subtle body of Mahadevī. The fourteen goddesses of this cakra are personifications of the fourteen principal *nāḍīs* (channels of psychic force) of Kuṇḍalinī Yoga and belong to the subtle body of both macrocosm and microcosm manifesting the identity of the two. In addition, they are the "fourteen instruments" of the Devī. These are the five sense organs; the five organs of action; *manas, buddhi, ahaṁkara* and *citta* (individual consciousnes). All but *citta* of these fourteen are among the thirty-six tattvas that belong both to macrocosm and microcosm. Again, in perceiving these identities the aspirant comes closer to the goal of oneness with Mahādevī, and through Her, oneness with the Ultimate Reality, the non-dual Brahman.

Sarvārthasādaka ("Accomplisher of all Aims"), the fifth cakra. This is the outer cakra of ten triangles. The ten deities here, called yoginīs, are *devatās* of auspiciousness. They are the objects of the sense organs and organs of action of the Great Goddess and are adorned with white garments and jewels. The Commentary on this passage in the *Kāmakalā-Vilāsa* explains, that the yoginīs "are objects of sense perception such as sound is of hearing and the like."[15] The Introduction to the *Tantrarāja Tantra* adds that the ten deities are also goddesses of the ten *prāṇas* which "are controlled by their worship."[16] Since the *prāṇas* are of the utmost importance in Tantric and all forms of yoga, the assistance of these deities is a boon to the aspirant in his quest for the *samādhi* of oneness with the One.

Sarvarakṣākara ("Giver of all Protection"), the fourth cakra. This is the inner cakra of ten triangles. In this area, the *sādhaka* approaches the full radiance of the Mahāśakti. The ten deities of the third, the next cakra, spread themselves "lighted by the light of Cit" as two divine lights; one shines forth in this the inner cakra of ten triangles, the other in the outer cakra of ten triangles in the fifth, the preceding cakra. The ten deities of this fourth cakra are again aspects of the vital sheath and have a twofold function: (1) they are auspicious powers; (2) they are functions of the vital fire (*vahnikalā*) that digests food of all kinds, a very human function that brings out the minute correspondences between macrocosm amd microcosm.

Sarvarogahara ("All Disease Destroyer"), the third cakra. In this cakra, the aspirant sees a vision of the eight deities of speech, lustrous with rays of light emanating from the central triangle. Also important for his effort towards self-realization is the significance of these goddesses as the *dvandvas* (pairs of opposites), cold-heat, pleasure-pain, desire and the guṇas. Since the Mind must do this, the mental sheath (this includes *buddhi*, *manas* and *ahaṁkara*) of the *sādhaka* functions here and parallels the mental sheath of the macrocosm.

Sarvasiddhiprada, the second cakra, the Kāmakalā Triangle. The name of the cakra means "that which accomplishes all, " for it is the first and innermost triangle with the Mahābindu in its center. This cakra is a tremendous experience for the aspirant. Here he is very close to the core of Reality, the Mahābindu, Source of Being, in all its radiant glory. We have already described the nature of the Kāmakalā triangle in the preceding chapters. Most important is that all the letters of the alphabet appear here; this means all sound (*śabda*) whence are derived all created things.

In the Kāmakalā triangle, the parallels offered between the aspirant as microcosm and the macrocosm are many. Each of the *kūṭas* of the Mahāmantra occupies a corner of the triangle, bringing out the equivalence between the Mahāmantra as sound-body of the Great goddess and her form-body, the Śrī Cakra. Both represent the entire cosmic reality in all its aspects, including the thirty-six *tattvas* of which everything in the universe is composed. Some of the most significant *tattvas* are specifically symbolized: *prakṛti, buddhi, ahaṁkara, manas* and the *tanmātras*. Such feelings and emotions as love and hate, attraction and repulsion also are represented, control over which aids the devotee in his attainment of self-realization.

The *pīṭhas* sacred to Mahādevi within this cakra are full of meaning for the aspirant because they bring out forcefully the divine status of the guru, namely, that the Śrī Cakra and the guru are the same. The lineage of the Gurus who teach the Vidyā begins with the Ādi-nātha or Ādi-guru, Śiva of the Kṛta Yuga (the Golden Age), continues through the great Gurus (or Nāthas) of the Treta, Dvāpara and Kali Yugas and then passes on to other teachers in a continuous stream called *ogha*.[17] Within the three classes of the *ogha* stream there is a triple relationship like that between the *sādhaka* and his guru. The *sādhaka* pays obeisance to his guru, the guru to his guru, and the guru of the latter, like the devotional pattern of father, grandfather, greatgrandfather. Since this pattern prevails in the three classes of the *ogha* stream we have what is called the Guru Maṇḍala of the Nava Nāthas (Nine Masters).[18] The number nine is thought significant because there are nine cakras in the Śrī Yantra which again shows the identity between the Guru and the Mahāyantra. Most important of all, however, is that the Guru follows in the wake of the *ogha* stream; it is primarily this that gives him divine status and empowers him to initiate the aspirant into the spiritual rebirth which gives him a body capable of receiving the divine. The *Bhavanopaniṣad* asserts that the Guru as the Nava Nāthas creates for the *sādhaka* the body with nine apertures because it is only through these sensory openings that the Divine may be received.[19] In the *ogha* stream the highest class, the Divya, forms the two ears and the mouth, the Siddha class the two eyes and genitals, the Mānava class the two nostrils and anus.[20] Through these sensory organs divinized by the Gurus as the Nava Nāthas, the *sādhaka* sees the identity between himself and the Mahāyantra. All this has come to him under the guidance of his Guru, who, as we said, is divine because he is part of the *ogha* stream originating with the Ādi Nātha, Śiva or Śakti. (In some Tantras Śiva is the Guru, in others Śakti.) Ultimately the two are One in non-dual union, the Brahman, so the Ādi Nātha is really Śiva-Śakti, the One Light, the Truth, the Ādi-Vidyā that illuminates the *ogha* stream and all Gurus who perceive their identity with the One. The aspirant through his divine rebirth perceives this divinity in his Guru and in himself and knows that both are one with the Śrī Cakra which is Śakti or Śiva-Śakti, the Universe both material and spiritual and the transcendent Brahman, the One. Then he goes on to the ultimate experience signified by the symbols in the innermost cakra.

Sarvānandamaya, the first and innermost cakra. This is the place of the Mahābindu, seat of Mahāśakti Herself where She is in blissful union with Śiva. The aspirant merges himself into this divine union, but must go beyond to the Nirguṇa Brahmān within the void that is beyond the Mahābindu, to realize his identity with the Two-in-One, the One that transcends the space-time world.[21]

Although liberation is possible by this method called Outer Worship, stage by stage through the nine cakras, most of the followers of the Tantric way to liberation look upon it as generally unsatisfactory. Preferred is the way of Inner Worship although it is much more difficult. This method centers upon the Śrī Cakra within the individual, the microcosm. Thus the primary Tantric method of self-realization involving the cakras within the individual that together correspond with the macrocosmic Śrī Cakra is Kuṇḍalinī Yoga.

NOTES

1. Arthur Avalon, trans., *Kāma-Kalā-Vilāsa* by Puṇyānanda-Nātha (Madras: Ganesh & Co. Pvt. Ltd., 1961) v. 21, p. 43.
2. *Ibid.*
3. *Lalitā-Sahasranāman*, *op. cit.*, p. 60.
4. *Ibid.*
5. *Ibid.*, p. 61.
6. *Ibid.*, p. 61 f.
7. *Ibid.*, p. 62.
8. W. Norman Brown, ed. *Saundaryalaharī*, Harvard Oriental Series, Vol. 43 (Cambridge : Harvard University Press, 1958), p. 6.
9. *Ibid.*, pp. 19-24.
10. *Śakta Upaniṣads*, *op. cit.*, p. 67. notes 1 and 4.
11. *Ibid.*, p. 68.
12. Sir John Woodroffe, *The Tantrarāja Tantra* (Madras: Ganesh & Co., 1954), p. 9.
13. *Kāmakalā-Vilāsa*, *op. cit.*, Commentary on v. 32, p. 60.
14. In the Upaniṣads we have our first formulation of the sheaths of the ātman and brahman; see Part I, Ch. III, the paragraphs on the Taittirīya Upaniṣad. In later Tantric (and Advaita Vedānta philosophy) the sheaths are

    1. *annamaya*, the gross body of material elements; 2. the *prāṇamaya*, the sheath of breath, the vital sheath; 3. the manomaya, the lower mental sheath of the lower mind and its organs of perception and action; 4. the *vijñānamaya*, the intellect which includes *buddhi* and is the higher mind; and 5. *ānandamaya*, the sheath of bliss.
15. *Kāmakalā-Vilāsa*, *op. cit.*, Commentary v. 42, p. 80.
16. Woodroffe, *Tantrarājā Tantra*, *op. cit.*, p. 8.
17. *Kāmakalā-Vilāsa*, *op. cit.*, vv. 52, 53, p. 94 and Commentary, p. 95.

18. S. Shankanarayan, *Śrī Cakra.* sec. ed. (Pondicherry: Dipti Publications, Sri Aurobindo Ashram, 1973), pp. 74f.
19. *Śakta Upaniṣads, op. cit., Bhavanopaniṣad*, p. 67 and Shankaranarayan, *ibid.*, p. 75.
20. Shankaranarayan, *Śrī Cakra, ibid.*, p. 75.
21. For a fuller account of this ultimate experience see the next chapter, "Kuṇḍalinī Yoga," the section on the Sahsrāra Cakra.

VI

KUṆḌALINI YOGA AND MACRO-MICROCOSMIC IDENTITY

Kuṇḍalinī yoga is the most richly symbolic, colorful and dramatic way of realizing the identity of the self as microcosm, with the Self of the Macrocosm. It is a method practiced not only by Tantrics in India today, but has also become known in the West where teachers of this yoga such as Muktananda have been influential.[1]

The process of realizing the identity between macrocosm and microcosm in this yoga, centers upon a step by step procedure up a series of psychic centers, the cakras or lotuses. The number of lotus petals assigned each cakra represents the *nāḍīs*, or channels of psychic force which meet at each cakra. Although their total number varies in the Tantric works,[2] there is agreement that the main ones are fourteen and chief among these are *Īḍā*, *Piṅgalā* and *Suṣumnā* identified respectively with the Sun, Moon and Fire. The Suṣumnā lies in the center of the cerebro-spinal axis. The spinal vertebral column itself is called the Mount Meru of the body, another macro-microcosmic identity. *Īḍā* begins at the left of it at the Mūlādhāra Cakra, while Piṅgalā is at the right of the same cakra. These *nāḍīs* wind around the cakras in the region of the spinal column from right to left and left to right in a pattern similar to the caduceus of the god Mercury, until they reach the Ājñā Cakra whence they proceed to the nostrils. In this way the psychic force courses through the cakras.

The central artery of this force, the Suṣumnā, contains within itself three other *nāḍīs*. The Suṣumnā is assigned the *tamas* as its predominant *guṇa* and fiery red as its color; Within it is the Vajriṇī *nāḍī* of lustrous hue with *rajas* as its predominant *guṇa*; and within Vajriṇī is the Citriṇī *nāḍī*, pale in color with the *sattva guṇa* predominant. Finally the Brahma-*nāḍī* begins at the lower end of Citrini, the place called the Brahma-dvara, and extends all the way upward to the Sahasrāra. It is through this *nāḍī* that kuṇḍalinī must be coaxed through the cakras to meet Paramaśiva in the Sahasrāra.

Before we delve into the journey of the aspirant through the cakras, it is important to realize that these cakras exist for the Tantric at the macrocosmic level as well as the microcosmic.

The Six Cakras of the Macrocosm. These are depicted most delightfully in a famous early poem, the *Saundaryalaharī*. Professor Norman Brown is of the view that this poem "presents an earlier and simpler form of Tantric Śaktism,"[3] and dates the work sometime after 1000 A.D. In this poem, the Six Cakras and the Sahasrāra are described as parts of Mahādevī as the macrocosmic Being, a Mahāpuruṣa that comprises within Herself the spiritual and material universe. She is the "cosmic woman who consists of the three worlds...".[4] The poet author lauds Her as mind, space, the wind, fire, the cosmic waters, the earth and supreme consciousness (*paracit*).[5] He describes her ascents and descents along the *kula* path as the cycles of dissolution and recreation of the universe. In the cycle of dissolution, she begins from the Mūlādhāra and ascends through the rest of the Six Cakras dissolving each center in turn (each is a part of the cosmos) until she reaches the Sahasrāra (the thousand-petalled lotus) where blissfully she joins Śiva in non-dual union. When the time is ripe, she begins another re-creation cycle which the poet portrays grandly. Another interesting feature of this poem is the subordination of Śiva to Devī's power contrary to the usual relationship of the pair in Tantric thought.

In this poem there is no mention of an identity between the macrocosm and the microcosm. The Sahasrāra and Six Cakras are described only as parts of Mahādevī. Therefore kuṇḍalinī yoga is not mentioned in this work. The Tantrics, however, assume this correlation of the Cakras between macrocosm and microcosm as it is indeed another prime example of their identity.

The Process of Ascent of the Yogin Through the Six Cakras to the Sahasrāra

Before he is qualified to begin the ascent of the cakras, the aspirant must observe certain preliminary disciplines similar to those required in Patañjali's classical yoga. These are the following:

1. *Yama* (Restraints). As in Patañjali's yoga the aspirant must observe *ahiṁsā* (non-injury to others), truthfulness, continence, non-stealing, compassion, fortitude, forbearance, straightforwardness, moderation in diet and general moral purity.[6]

2. *Niyama* (Observances). The devotee must observe certain virtues or regulations. These are contentment, austerity (*tapas*), belief in and worship of God, prayer, modesty, sacrifice, and listening to the teaching of Vedāntic doctrines.[7]

3. *Āsanas* (Postures). Postures of the body must be learned for health, and mastery over these is required to free the mind for the concentration essential in this yoga. As many as eighty-four postures are described in the *Haṭhayogapradīpikā*, but all are not of equal importance. The greatest according to this and another authoritative work, the *Śiva Saṁhitā*, is the *Siddha*. The yogin takes this position: He presses the perineum with the base of the left heel and places the other foot above the genital organ. His chin is kept on his breast. He must remain motionless with the sense-organs under full control and steadily fix his eyes upon the spot between the eyebrows.[8]

Another *āsana* of great importance is *prāṇayāma* which the Tantrics refer to as *kumbhaka*. This is restraint of the breath. As in Patañjali's yoga, the aspirant must learn to hold his breath for progressively longer periods since this is the greatest of all aids in attaining the ultimate experience of oneness with the One. To understand better the significance of *praṇa* in this yoga, we should know that the ultimate purpose of practice of the Kumbhakas as well as of the Āsanas and Mudrās (see below) is the forcing of the Prāṇa out of the main *Nāḍīs*, Īḍā and Piṅgalā, to have it enter the Suṣumnā.[9] The methods employed must force the *Prāṇa* (the upward breath) downward and the *Apana* (the downward breath) upward. Thus, these powerful Prāṇas, entrapped without escape, generate so much heat that Kuṇḍalinī is aroused and enters the Brahma-dvāra.[10] This is the door, the entrance to the Suṣumnā from the Mūlādhāra. From here, Kuṇḍalinī may enter the Suṣumnā and pierce some or all of the Cakras, according to the competence of the yogin. Also "when the breath flows through the Suṣumnā the mind becomes steady,"[11] which is essential for the intense concentration that leads to samādhi. Thus restraint of the breath is of utmost importance in this yoga. The *Haṭhayogapradīpikā* describes nine, but the one called Kevala Kumbhaka is first among them all, a state "without inhalation or exhalation, when the breath is retained with ease."[12]

4. *Mudrās*. Another great aid in arousing Kuṇḍalinī is the practice of Mudrās. Greatest among these is said to be the *Khecari* because it is

such a great aid in attaining Kevala Kumbhaka. To perform this Mudrā, the tongue must be elongated sufficiently to turn back and enter the roof of the palate, closing off air to the throat. Meanwhile, the eyes must be centered upon a point between the eyebrows. However, one must beware of holding the breath too long as this may result in insensibility. Needless to say, this and all the disciplines in this yoga must be undertaken only under the guidance of a qualified guru.

Another significant Mudrā is the *Yoni* whereby one may attain the samādhi of Liberation. Before beginning this Mudrā, the yogin performs the Śakticālana Mudrā which has as its main feature the movement of the abdominal muscle from right to left and left to right in a spiraline manner to arouse the sleeping Kuṇḍalinī and cause her to rise up. Then the yogin assumes the Siddhāsana posture and closes all the apertures in his head : the ears with his thumbs, eyes with his index finger, upper lip with his ring-fingers, and the lower with his little fingers.[13] This done, he draws in the prāṇa very slowly and unites it with Apāna. Next he contemplates the Six Cakras beginning with Mūlādhāra, while repeating the mantra *Huṁ Haṁsah*. Huṁ signifies *kāma* (desire) and *krodha* anger. In this context, *kāma* refers to *sṛṣṭi* (creation) and *krodha* to dissolution (*laya*); the latter refers to destroyer gods, aspects of Śakti as Destroyer at the end of the *kalpa*. The Haṁ of Haṁsah stands for Purusa and the Sah for Prakṛti, the basic components of Macrocosm and Microcosm.[14] In these ways the aspirant identifies himself with Śakti-Kuṇḍalinī and thinks upon the blissful union of Śakti with Śiva in the Sahasrāra.

The above account of some of the most significant *āsanas*, *kumbhakas* and *mudrās* completes the more physical aspects of the disciplines the *sādhaka* may need to undergo in order to arouse kuṇḍalinī and continue with Her the often difficult spiritual journey through the Cakras to ultimate Liberation.This journey is his arduous ascent of the Six Cakras to the Sahasrāra.

Macro-Microcosmic Symbols in the Yogin's Ascent of the Six Cakras and the Sahasrāra

The process of ascent of the Six Cakras in Kuṇḍalinī Yoga, also known as *Laya yoga*, is concerned with the internal, the subtle body, specifically with its *nāḍīs*, especially Īḍā, Piṅgalā and Suṣumnā, and above all with the Six Cakras and the Sahasrāra. In Laya yoga the aspirant sheds the layers of his gross and subtle bodies until he attains his original state of identity with the One, the non-dual Śiva-Śakti or Brahman. As we saw in the preceding chapter, the Śrī Cakra is the outward symbol of the evolutionary and involutionary process of the macrocosmic reality, and meditation upon this symbol is a major aid in reintegration of the yogin; but the more spiritually mature may skip this step and concern themselves with the inner Śrī Cakra, the Six Cakras and the Sahasrāra. The Six Cakras are known as the Lower Śrī Cakra; the Sahasrāra as the Upper Śrī Cakra; and both together are the Śrī Cakra within the yogin himself as microcosm and manifest his identity with the macrocosm.

We are now ready to take the involutionary journey from Cakra to Cakra whereby the yogin sheds both his gross and subtle bodies and becomes one with the Absolute Reality This journey is taken under the close supervision of a qualified guru in whom the aspirant has complete faith and follows as if he were the Ādi-Guru, Śiva, himself.

Mūlādhāra Cakra (or Lotus). This, the first of the Six Cakras, is in the region below the genitals and above the anus. It is in the form of the square and has four lotus petals around it, one on each side. The square is the form of the *tattva* or element "earth." Each Cakra contains a particular number of *tattvas* so that all are included within the six, an identity between macrocosm and microcosm. The lower *tattvas* are in the lower cakras, the higher *tattvas* in the higher Cakras. Other tattvas included in this Cakra correlated with the low level of "earth" are *gandha* (odor), one of the Tanmātras; the sense organ "smell," and "feet," one of the Karmendriyas.

On each of the four lotus petals around the square region, yellow in color (the color of earth), there is a letter. These, reading from left to right are: va, śa, ṣa, sa. The lotus petals of each cakra contain certain letters so that all the letters of the Sanskrit alphabet are contained within the six. As we have seen in previous chapters, this represents the entire world of *śabda* whence issues the entire universe. This again identifies the microcosm with the macrocosm.

In the center of the yellow square we see the *bīja* (seed syllable) of this Cakra, *Lam*, seated on an elephant. Within the *bindu* of the *bīja* we find the god, Brahmā, the presiding diety. Each Cakra also has its Śakti or Queen, the deity of the *dhātu* of the Center. The *dhātus*, as we said above, are components of the body. Here the Śakti of the *dhātu*, bone, is *Dākinī*, who functions here also as "carrier of the revelation of the ever-pure Intelligence."[15] This means that through meditation on her the yogin acquires knowledge of this Cakra.

THE SIX CAKRAS

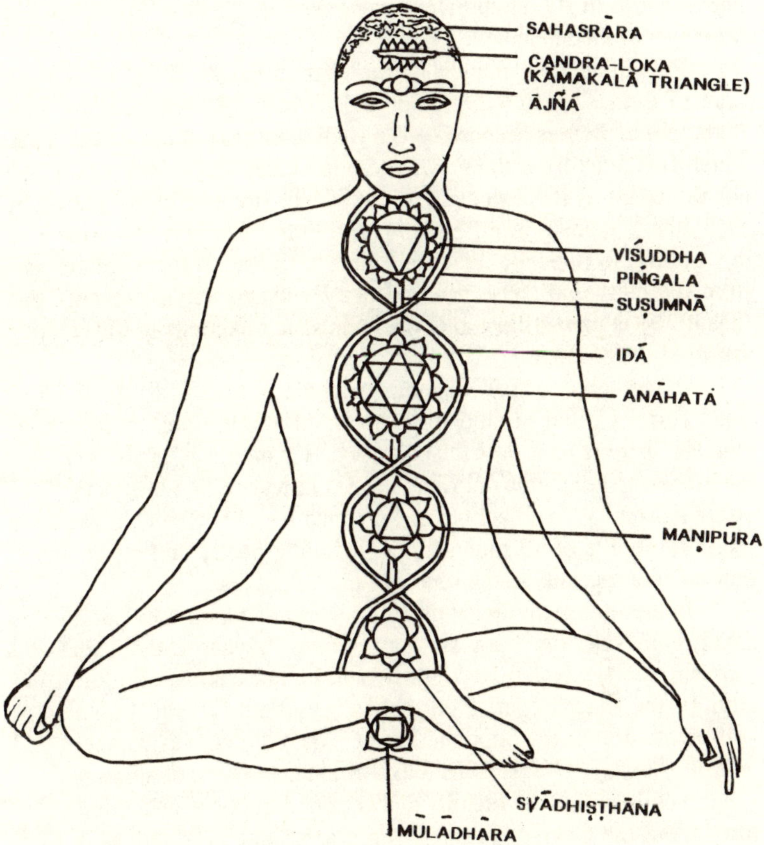

Diagram III

Within the very center of the square is the luminous "lightning-like triangle which is Kāmarūpa and known as *Traipura*."[16] It is called the Śakti Pīṭha because of the presence of the Devi Tripurasundarī in the Ka of the triangle. Ka is the first letter of the Kāmakuṭā (or Kāma-bīja) the first part of the Pañcadaśākṣarī Mantra. The lines of the triangle are called Vāma, Jyeṣṭhā and Raudrī as in the Kāmakalā in the Sahasrāra, so the Traipura is known as the lower Kāmakalā Triangle. These deities of the Traipura represent Devī as Creator, Preserver and Destroyer of the universe.

Pervading this triangle is the Vāyu or Breath called *Kandarpa*, Lord of Beings, deep red in color and glowing like ten millions suns. He is lord of Beings because he is a significant part of the Apāna Vāyu which functions from the anus. The other chief Vāyu is Prāṇa which has the Heart as its center. These two vāyus are constantly pulled by each other, Apāna upward by Prāṇa and Prāṇa downward by Apāna. If this pulling in opposite directions were to cease, Prāṇa would escape from the body and cause death. Since Kandarpa Vāyu prevents this (death), he is named Lord of Life, and as such belongs to the creative aspect of the cosmos.

In the center of the Kāmarūpa triangle is Śiva as Svayambhū in linga form. Coiled around him three-and-a-half times is Kuṇḍalinī Herself lustrous as a flash of lightning. Her mouth is pressed against the Brahma-dvāra thereby closing off the entrance of the Suṣumnā. "Her sweet murmur is like the hum of love-mad bees."[17] She is, as we have seen, the source of all sound-forms including poetry and music and is praised here specially as the source of these delights.

In the four great divisions of the world of *śabda*, Devī is, in this cakra, Parā-Vāk, the Parā state of *śabda*. Paśyanti, Madhyamā and Vaikharī *śabdas* which we shall find in higher cakras, all issue from Her. In the macrocosm, Parā Śabda originates in the bursting or "differentiation of the Supreme Bindu" when "there was unmanifested 'sound' (Śabda)."[18] This is the Śabda-Brahman, source of all sound.

Another kind of identity between macrocosm and microcosm throughout the Cakras is that of Space and Time. The tattvas of each cakra have a definite number of rays totaling 365, the number of days in the year, and the year from the time of the Brāhmaṇas is the symbol of Time. The Mūlādhāra has 56 of the rays. The correspondence in Space between macro- and microcosm is precise : the regions below the Mūlādhāra are equated with the seven lower worlds of the macrocosm; the Mūlādhāra itself with the earth-surface called Bhūrloka; and the five upper cakras in succession, with the six regions above the earth. The cosmos has become far more complex than the "three worlds" of Vedic times.

Knowing all these identities between himself as microcosm and the macrocosm, the yogin is now told to meditate upon Devī Kuṇḍalinī who is Creator, Preserver and Destroyer, beyond the universe, is consciousness itself and the "One who goes upwards."[19] Then he must arouse Kuṇḍalinī so that he can get through the Brahma-dvāra, the door to the Suṣumnā, the main channel through which he must travel to reach each of the cakras. It is especially difficult to do this at this cakra, because in the Mūlādhāra, is one of the three Granthis (knots) where *māyā* is especially strong. At these places, Śakti and Śiva are united; here Śakti as Kuṇḍalinī is coiled around the Śiva lingam.

With the aid of the Āsanas, Kumbhakas and Mudrās described above, and the kind of meditation recommended, the aspirant must arouse Kuṇḍalinī with whom he identifies himself. If successful, with Her he begins the ascent of the succeeding cakras. He leaves behind in the Mūlādhāra all of its *tattvas* which are now all dissolved.

Svādiṣṭhāna Cakra (or Lotus). Continuing upward the yogin enters the Svādiṣṭhāna Cakra located in the region, vermillion in color, inside the Suṣumnā at the root of the genitals. It has six petals with letters in lightning-like form: Baṁ, Bhaṁ, Maṁ, Yaṁ, Raṁ, Laṁ. Thus the world of sound is illustrated here, but now in its Paśyanti state, the state characterized by general movement. This state extends up to the Maṇipūra Cakra. In the microcosm its center is also here in the Svadiṣṭhāna Lotus.

In the pericarp of this Cakra is the white region of water, an area in the shape of a crescent, the form of the element (*bhūta*) water, Within the crescent is the *bīja* of the god, Varuṇa, *Vaṁ*, also white in color. The *bīja* is seated on a *makara* (a mythical creature, perhaps a dolphin), the vehicle of the god, Varuṇa. The yogin is to meditate upon the *bīja*, Vaṁ. Above the *bīja* is the Bindu within which is the presiding *devatā* of the Cakra, Viṣṇu, deep blue in color and with four arms, seated upon his vehicle, Garuḍa. The yogin is to meditate upon both Varuṇa and Viṣṇu. The Śakti of the Cakra is Rākiṇī, goddess of the dhātu, fat.

In relation to Time, the tattva water, of this center has 62 rays of the total of 365 which complete the Year. In relation to Space, this area in the microcosm corresponds with the Bhūvarloka (atmosphere-heaven) of the macrocosm.

The *tattvas* of *prakṛti* dissoved here are : the *bhūta*, water; the sense-organ taste; the *tanmātra*, generic essence of taste; the *karmendriya*, hands.

When the aspirant passes successfully this cakra, he ascends with Kuṇḍalini to the Maṇipurā Lotus.

Maṇipurā Cakra. This is in the region of the navel. It has ten petals of the color of "heavy-laden rain-clouds." The ten letters of the alphabet each with bindu are : Ḍaṁ, Ḍhaṁ, Naṁ, Taṁ, Thaṁ, Daṁ Dhaṁ, Naṁ, Paṁ, Phaṁ.

The yogin is to meditate here on the region of Fire represented by a large triangle that shines "like the rising sun." Within the triangle is the *bīja* of Fire, Raṁ, seated on a ram, vehicle of Agni, god of Fire. In the "lap" of the *bīja* is the deity who presides over this Cakra, *Rudra*, a form of Śiva as Destroyer, seated on the bull, *Nandi*. In appearance he is old, to symbolize his function as Destroyer at the end of the world cycle. Here also is the Śakti of the Cakra, *Lākinī*, who represents the *dhātu*, "flesh," and is called "benefactress of all," no doubt because with Rudra she symbolizes the Destroyer phase of the world cycle, the beneficient phase for the yogin who yearns for dissolution into the Primeval One.

Time is represented by the number of rays, 52, of the tattva, Fire; space and its identity with the macrocosm by the correspondence of this Lotus with the Svarloka, the Heaven where Indra and other gods dwell.

In this Cakra, further progress towards dissolution is made by the shedding of many more of the grosser tattvas: the *bhūta*, fire; the *tanmātra*, essence of color or form; the sense-organ, sight, and the *karmendriya*, the anus.

As the yogin, identified with Kuṇḍalinī , ascends the Cakras, their respective lotuses "bloom," *i.e.* they lift their petals upward which before were hanging downward. This symbolizes the yogin's progress towards the Light, the Source of Being, the One. When the yogin leaves a cakra, the petals again return to the downward-hanging position. This means turning away from the One to the Many, the created multiple world. Another phenomenon characteristic of the ascent through the Cakras is the coldness of the parts of the body that Kuṇḍalinī and the yogin leave behind in their ascent. Finally at the Sahasrāra, the yogin is very cold throughout his entire body except at the top of his head, the region of the Sahasrāra.

To return to the Maṇipūra Cakra, the *sādhka*, after having meditated there, strives to enter a still more potent and beautiful region, that of the Anāhata Lotus.

The Anāhata Cakra. This is in the heart region and is red in color. The name means "unstruck," called thus because here the sound of *śabda brahman* is heard, a sound "which issues without the striking of any two things together."[20] In the macrocosm, we have seen the Śabda-Brahman equated with the Prāṇava, OṀ, and the Kāmakalā Triangle, Upon the hearing of this sound, the yogin is ready to proceed to the higher meditative states in the upper cakras that lead to Liberation.

Also of importance in relation to Śabda, this Cakra is the seat of Madhyamā Śabda located in the region from the Maṇipurā to this Cakra. Madhyamā Śabda belongs to the world of the subtle or mental body (sukṣma śarīra). In this world, there is mental cognition of mental representations of objects, that is, an idea-world and its organs of cognition. Another aspect of Śabda here, as in all six Cakras, is the inclusion of letters of the alphabet, one for each petal of the 12-petalled lotus. These are : ka, kha, ga, gha, ṅa, ca, cha, ja, jha, ña, ṭa, ṭha.

In the pericarp of this lotus is the Vāyu maṇḍala, hexagonal in form and smoky in color, made by two intersecting triangles, one male and one female, with apexes pointing, respectively, upward and downward. The hexagon is the form of the tattva, air, the reigning one here. In the center is the *bīja* of Air, *Yaṁ*, with four arms and seated on a black antelope. The reigning god of the Cakra is *Īśa*, a form of Śiva. He is within the hexagonal form seated in the lap of the *bīja*, Yaṁ. He is poetically described as "the beautiful One possessed of the soft radiance of ten million moons, and shining with the radiance of his matted hair."[21] The Śakti of Śiva is also here in the pericarp of this Lotus in the form of a Trikoṇa (the female triangle). Within this Trikoṇa is Śiva in the form of the Bāṇa Liṅga. As we noted above, these cakras where Śiva and Śakti are together are granthiṣṭhānas, difficult for the yogin to pass through.

The Śakti of the *dhātu*, blood, is *Kākinī*, three-eyed like Śiva. She is called "benefactress of all."

Immediately below the Heart Lotus is a lesser eight-petalled lotus which is the seat of the aspirant's *iṣṭadevatā* (patron deity). Here the yogin performs mental worship of, and meditation upon this deity for help and strength to pass through this very difficult cakra. When he is successful, he rids himself of several more of the tattvas: the essence-of-touch *tanmātra*; the *bhūta*, air; the sense-organ touch; the *karmendriya*, the reproductive organ. In the next Cakra, the Viśuddha, he will dissolve the remaining grosser tattvas of *prakṛti*.

Time is manifested in this region in the number of rays, 54, of the tattava, Vāyu, i.e., 54 days of the year of 360 days.

The identity in space between microcosm and macrocosm is shown in the correspondence between the region of the Anāhata Lotus with the Mahā-loka, the heavenly sphere where saints live for an entire kalpa (complete world cycle of 4,320,000,000 years). The yogin, like these saints, must reach a high degree of spiritual perfection in this Cakra, sufficient to lead Kuṇḍalinī through this difficult *granthiṣṭhāna*, on to the Viśuddha Cakra.

The Viśuddha Cakra. This Lotus, located in the throat region, has sixteen petals of a smoky purple hue. Each is inscribed in red with a vowel of the Sanskrit alphabet ending with bindu. These are : a, ā, i, ī, u, ū, ṛ, ṝ, ḷ, ḹ, e, o, ai, au, aṁ, aḥ. Bindu is added to all the vowels except the two breathings aṁ, and aḥ (or ah:) This is the total number of vowels in the Sanskrit alphabet. In relation to Śabda in general, this is the region of Vaikharī Śabda *i.e.* of gross overt speech, for here are the vocal cords and mouth, organs of speech.

In the pericarp of the Lotus is the maṇḍala of Ether (*ākāśa*) purest and finest of all the gross tattvas, represented in the form of a white circle. Within it is the *bīja* of Ether, *haṁ*, which is also white and mounted on a white elephant. The god of the Cakra is Sadāśiva in his Ardhanārīśvara form (half male and half female). He is seated in the lap of the *bīja*. On the left side, he is golden in color and female to represent the Divine as Śakti; on the right side, he is white and male as Śiva. This androgynous symbol brings out the equal significance of these aspects of God, not yet merged into the non-dual Brahman. Sadāśiva is on a lion-seat placed on the back of a bull, Śiva's vehicle.

The Śakti of the *dhātu*, which is bone, is *Sākinī*, garbed in yellow. The yogin is directed to meditate on her who is "light itself." Contemplation in this Cakra brings the aspirant peace of mind, eloquence and wisdom. His wisdom includes knowledge of all Time— present, past and future. The totality of time is also represented here in the microcosm by the number of rays assigned to each tattva, 72 of the 360 days that make the year.

The identity between microcosm and macrocosm in Space is brought out in the correspondence between this Cakra and the Janaloka, the heavenly sphere of the pure-minded, the patriarchs and progenitors of mankind.

The yogin who is successful in coaxing Kuṇḍalinī to unite with his own *Jīvātman* through this Cakra dissolves the rest of the grosser tattvas, which are the *bhūta*, *ākāśa*; the *tanmātra*, essence-of-sound; the sense-organ, hearing; the karmendriya, the mouth.

The Ājñā Cakra. The yogin has now reached the last, the sixth cakra, the one which prepares him for the ultimate experience in the Sahasrāra. The name, Ājñā, means "command" signifying in this context that the command of the guru is received from above.[22] The Guru is Śiva Himself and seen as Paramaśiva in his Cakra, but pre-eminently above in the Sahasrāra. The Ājñā cakra is also called Mukta-triveṇi because it is the place where the three great nāḍīs--Īḍā, Piṅgalā and Suṣumnā—go forth separately, each with its own function and location described at the beginning of this chapter. The macrocosmic *triveṇi* is the juncture of the three great sacred rivers, Gaṅgā, Yamunā and the "underground" Sarasvatī. This is another of the many homologisms which show the likeness between the microcosm and the macrocosm.

The Ājñā Lotus is located between and behind the eyebrows. Its two petals, white like the moon, has each a letter variegated in color; these are *Ha* and *Kṣa*. This completes the enitre Sanskrit alphabet. Since, as we have repeatedly noted, each letter is a mantra and all sounds are included in the letters of the alphabet and their combinations, the totality of all objects in the universe— the entire macrocosm—is represented in the six Cakras.

The *bīja* in the circular pericarp of this Lotus is OṀ, the most celebrated mantra in Hinduism. The "O" of OṀ, as we said in Part I, is composed of the letters "A" and "U" which is Sanskrit become "O"; a crescent moon symbolizing *nāda* is placed over the "O"; over the crescent is the dot that means "M" as bindu; over bindu is placed a half-crescent called the second nāda. The latter signifies "part of the differentiating *parabindu* placed above the *praṇava*."[23]

OṀ is called the abode of Śakti, therefore portrayed within the Śakti triangle which has the apex pointing down ward. Śiva, too, is here within the triangle in liṅga form called Itāra. This makes this Cakra another of the *granthisṭhānas*, the places most difficult for the yogin to penetrate.

The Śakti of the Cakra, *Hākinī*, of the *dhātu*, marrow, is seated on a white lotus. She, too, is white and has six faces shining like the moon.

The tattvas here are the subtle ones, *manas* and the subtle primary *prakṛti*. *Manas* in this context refers not only to the lower mind, ordinarily designated manas, but includes also the higher mental functions *ahaṁkara* and *buddhi*.

The yogin's main purpose in this region is to rid himself of the subtle tattvas just mentioned.To accomplish this, he is instructed to meditate upon the significant objects in the Cakra in the following order: first, Hākinī in the pericarp; then the Ītara Liṅga in the Trikoṇa; then the Praṇava and lastly Manas. Since the climax of the meditation is to get rid of the subtle tattvas, the yoga prescribed is called Praṇava Yoga, a discipline centered upon detaching the *manas* from its objects. The aspirant is advised to assume the Yoni-Mudrā (described above) as an aid. Meanwhile Kumbhaka is performed, retaining the air which is to be sipped through the lips. During this process the yogin should meditate on the Haṁsa or Ajapā Mantra to realize the unity of *prāṇa* and *manas*, i.e., the subtle tattvas of mind and subtle matter (*prakṛti*). The Haṁsa Mantra here is the breathing process itself. Breath as inspiration is Sa or Śakti and as expiration is Ha or Śiva. Thus we have the Mantra, Haṁsah, which, as the breathing process itself, done without volition, is also named the Ajapā (unuttered) Mantra. Performed here, it is evidently done as conscious meditation on the breathing in Khuṁbaka to realize the unity of *prāṇa* and *manas* to rid the meditator of both.

The Khecari Mudrā (described above) is also recommended to accomplish the same purpose as the Yoni-mudrā. By means of these *mudrās* the yogin, if successful, detaches the mind completely from all objects, thus from the world of *prakṛti*, including the subtle primary *prakṛti* of the three *guṇas*. *Manas* and *prakṛti* are then dissolved in the *citta* of pure consciousness and the state of *Unmanī* is reached. Unmani means literally "without mind" and signifies that the mental tattvas along with the subtle primary *prakṛti* have now been dissolved.

Having now shed all thirty-six of the tattvas, the yogin experiences great bliss. He sees sparks of Light surrounding the Praṇava. He also sees the light of Paramaśiva Himself, "the Light which is in the form of a flaming lamp. . . and glows between Sky and Earth."[24] Paramaśiva is here and also in the Sahasrāra. Śakti, too, is here with Śiva, both inseparably united in the Bindu of the Mantra OṀ, a paradigm in this cakra of the Parabindu in the Sahasrāra.[25]

This Cakra is so potent in attaining release from all tattvas and the availability of union with the One, the Brahman, represented in the Bindu of OṀ, that a yogin who feels he is about to die may gain release by placing his *prāṇa* in the Bindu of OṀ in this Cakra. Of course he must first take the journey we have described, merged in Kuṇḍalinī, through the five lower Cakras to rid himself of the grosser and the subtle tattvas, so that the mental components and the subtle *prakṛti* whence all originated are dissolved in the One, the non-dual Śiva-Śakti or Brahman of the Bindu of OṀ. This done, he "pierces the Brahmarandhra and leaves the body," now one with the One.[26] But ordinarily, the last and final stage in Kuṇḍalinī Yoga is entrance into the Sahasrāra Padma (Lotus).

Time appears in the microcosm in this Cakra in the number of rays assigned its tattva, *manas*, 64, i.e., 64 days of the Year, symbol of all Time. Identity between macrocosm and microcosm in Space is represented in the correspondence of this region in the microcosm with the heavenly region called the Tapoloka where the much-revered ascetics dwell.

If the yogin succeeds in passing through this difficult Cakra, he is ready to enter the most blissful of abodes, the goal of his entire spiritual journey, the Sahasrāra.

Sahasrāra Lotus. This is the Lotus-of-a-Thousand-Petals in the region at the top of the head. The petals hang downward. Between it and the Ājña Cakra is the causal body of the individual,[27] but between the Ājñā Cakra and the Sahasrāra there are seven intermediate causal forms[28] which we briefly defined in our chapter above on the Pañcadaśākarī Mantra. A fuller account follows. (1) Bindu. This is the Bindu of OṀ in the Ājñā Cakra described above. It is in Īśvara Tattva where all creation is in seed form. (2) Bodhinī in Sadāśiva Tattva wherein the duality of subject and object first appears. This power of Devī represents the stage of the limitation of the universality of the prior stage of Śakti called (3) Nāda which is also in the Sadāśiva Tattva. Here there is full equality of subject and object, the Aham and the Idam (the I and the This). Nāda is said to be the filling up of the whole universe with (4) Nadānta,[29] a causal form again in Sadāśiva Tattva. Nadānta is the going forth in "great strength" of the Śabda-Brahman in its Śiva form producing by its vibrations the first sound which resembles that of the bell. (5) Vyāpikā. This is in Śakti Tattva and is an aspect of Samanā Śakti (the next causal form) who is called Vyāpikā when she "withdraws into herself all thinkables which are her creation."[30] (6) Samanā who is also in Śakti Tattva. This is the stage in dissolution or creation of the universe in which Śakti exhibits Herself as the entire macrocosm composed of the tattvas, but in the form of thought. (7) Unmanī is in Śiva Tattva. Here there is complete subjectivity, no trace of objectivity until Śakti becomes active as Samanā. Thus when the yogin proceeds through the above causal stages and reaches Unmanī Avasthā, he has only to merge himself into the Causal Source of all Being, Parasaṁvit, the Śūnya in the Mahābindu of Kāmakalā Triangle in the Sahasrāra.

The Sahasrāra Lotus has a thousand white petals inscribed with the letters of the Sanskrit alphabet. These are the letters that the yogin with Kuṇḍalinī absorbed in the Six Cakras ascended in his spiritual journey. As we have said, these letters are potent because they are the constituents of the sound vibrations or mantras which concretize as the myriad objects of the universe. In the Sahasrāra each letter is multiplied twently times, so that we have a total of one-thousand, one letter on each of the thousand petals. This multiplication into one-thousand signifies, that the Sahasrāra is the place of the macrocosmic reality whose infinity, whose vastness of multiple worlds, contrasts sharply with the microcosmic world of the individual. As Woodroffe comments, "Haṁsa, Jīva or Kuṇḍalinī is but an infinitesimal part of the Parabindu."[31] Within the Parabindu (or Mahābindu) is the Śūnya (void) that is the Nirguṇa Brahman. The yogin's goal, if he wishes final liberation, is absorption into, union of identity with, the Nirguṇa Brahman.

The Parabindu is in the center of the Kāmakalā Triangle in the pericarp or the Candra-loka, the white lotus of twelve petals in the Sahasrāra. As we noted above in our chapter on the Śrī Yantra, the Kāmakalā is the core triangle of this celebrated Yantra which is the form of Śakti. The Kāmakalā Triangle in the Sahasrāra is the *sukṣma* (subtle) aspect of Tripura-Trikoṇa, the *sthūla* (gross) aspect of Śakti in the Mūlādhāra Cakra. As we said earlier, the Sahasrāra is known as the Upper Śrī Cakra and the six centers below as the Lower. Our investigation into the nature and content of these Cakras has shown that they are indeed like the Śrī Cakra, representations of the universe, of Devī Herself in this form.

The Candraloka is also called the *baindava-sthāna* (the place of the Bindu), the Upper Śrī Cakra and the "supreme city of Śrīvidyā," "outside and beyond the countless myriads of world systems, in the ocean of nectar."[32] This world of nectar is the *parabindu* in the center of the Candraloka where Paramaśiva and Śakti dwell in eternal union whence issues forth the divine nectar as the "ocean" of bliss. In support of this interpretation, a learned Tantric quoted by Woodroffe also speaks of the Candraloka as the world of nectar, for it is the place of union of *Sat* (Śiva as pure Being) and *Cit* (Śakti as Pure Consciousness).[33] Woodroffe, too, interprets the "ocean of nectar" as "the Infinite Consciousness Itself" and the gem-island (poetic name for Śrividyā's city in the ocean of nectar) as a "supreme state of consciousness."[34]

In the *baindava-sthāna* where Śiva and Śakti are ever united, both are above all tattvas and ever-shining with countless rays issuing forth from Śakti's being. These are the source of all the light in universes, and illumine the world as the sun, the moon and fire whence are derived the particular number of rays of each of the tattvas in the Six Cakras described above. Their total number, 360, we know comprise the Year of 360 days, symbol of all Time. These rays are, like their divine Source eternal and unlimited by space; the Candraloka is beyond the space-time worlds, although the Sahasrāra is identified with the Satya Loka of the Cosmos, the highest of heavens. It is the region of Truth where the holy ones are never reborn, but are absorbed into Brahman at the end of the enormously long, the many, many kalpas, of the 100-year life of the god, Brahmā, regent of this heaven.[35]

In the foregoing account of the Candraloka, Śakti has been given the dominant place. But Śiva is given equal, if not greater significance in works like the *Pādukā-Pañcaka*, (*The Fivefold Footstool*) said to have been written by Śiva himself.[36] In the commentary on the first verse of this work, the meaning of the twelve letters of the White-Petalled Lotus is explained as the Guru Mantra (sa, ha, kha, phreṁ, ha, sa, kṣa, ma, la, va, ra, yūṁ).

The Guru, Paramaśiva Himself, is within the Kāmakalā Triangle in the pericarp of the Twelve-Petalled Lotus, the place "where the two pericarps come together," the pericarps of the Sahasrāra and Twelve-Petalled Lotuses. In the pericarp of the latter is the Kāmakalā Triangle, the center triangle of the Śrī Cakra. Here we need to remind ourselves, that this triangle contains all the immense potentialities for the creation of myriads of universes, also for their preservation and dissolution. We should also recall that the Triangle itself emanates from the Mahābindu the Source of All, which is the place of Śiva and Śakti in union. The aspirant, in Śakti, enjoys the bliss of union with Śiva in the lake of nectar.

But the yogin seeking *mokṣa* does not stay in this blissful place. The Parabindu must be dissolved into the *Cidātma*, the supreme Nirguṇa Śiva (or Nirguṇa Brahman), the Ultimate Reality, the Cit (consciousness) which transcends yet pervades all. To do this, the sādhaka meditates upon Kuṇḍalinī as pure Cit. The Cidātma is in the void (*Śūnya*) within the Mahābindu. Concentrated meditation upon the truth that he is identical with the One, the Nirguṇa Brahman, infinite, eternal, and so beyond all attributes, brings him to vivid self-realization, to the direct experience of being actually, "One without a second," the Eternal Being (Sat), the Supreme Bliss (Ānanda), the Cidātma (the Supreme Consciousness), the Witness Self. This is the supreme, ineffable state, the ultimate self-realization that has been the goal of his arduous spiritual journey. He is now a *Jīvan-mukta* (one liberated while alive). His life-span is now limited to the time it takes to work out his past karma not yet exhausted. Meanwhile he can lead Kuṇḍalinī to the

Sahasrarā when he wishes, and gently bring her back again to the Mūlādhāra. He can foretell the time of his death, for he now possesses extraordinary powers. When this is about to occur, he ascends the Cakras to the Sahasrāra, becomes one with Brahman there, and leaves all forms of embodiment forever, to be eternally one with the One.

But before and during his *sādhana*, and before final release from the body, the Tantric yogin takes delight in the present world of persons. animals and objects because they are aspects of Śakti whose body is the universe. This joy in the world is called *bhukti*. Nevertheless, the yogin has chosen what he thinks is the supreme joy, *mukti* (*mokṣa*), the supreme transcendent bliss of becoming one with the macrocosmic One in its Eternal, Infinite aspect, the Two-in-One, Śakti and Śiva in non-dual union.

Kuṇḍalinī yoga is very much alive today. As we noted in our Introduction, the philosopher Sri Aurobindo thinks that the macrocosmic evolutionary process of the realization of Spirit is paralleled in the Yogin's experience in his ascension of the Six Cakras to the Sahasrāra where he enters the Gnostic level. Aurobindo also praises Tantric thought for another reason. This is because *bhukti*, delight in the world, as well as *mukti*, release and freedom from its limitations in oneness with the Self, the Eternal, are both emphasized as in Aurobindo's own philosophy.[37]

A similar viewpoint is held by the late Swami Muktananda, a respected tantric teacher of India who had recently been lecturing in United States. His yoga is described in his book *Play of Consciousness*. Muktananda's religious experience did not follow the precise pattern of the ascent of the Cakras described above, but essentially his experience was the same and ended with the philosophy of *bhukti* and *mukti*.[38]

One of the leaders of the new school of transcendental psychology, heavily influenced by Muktananda's book and his personality, accepts what he calls the principles of this Tantric teacher. These are (1) Freedom (*cf. mukti*), (2) Love, (*cf. bhukti*), and (3) Consciousness or awareness. By consciousness he means oneness with the Self or Absolute.[39]

Thus the ancient *tat tvam asi* of the Upaniṣads, the identity between macro and microcosm is the prime attainment to be realized. All else follows.

NOTES

1. See Swami Muktananda, *Play of Consciousness* (*Chitshakti Vilas*), (San Francisco: Harper & Row, 1974).
2. Avalon (Sir John Woodroffe), *The Serpent Power*, *op. cit.*, p. 110.
3. Norman Brown, *Saundaryalaharī*, *op. cit.*, Introduction, p. 24.
4. *Ibid.*, pp. 26-30.
5. *Ibid.*, *Saundaryalaharī*, v. 19. p. 54.
6. *The Haṭhayogapradīpikā of Svātmārāma*, with Commentary of Brahmānanda, translated by Srinivasa Iyangar (Madras : The Theosophical Publishing House, 1972, reprinted 1975), I. 16.
7. *Ibid.*
8. *Ibid.*, I.35.
9. Avalon, *The Serpent Power*, *op. cit.*, p. 230
10. *Ibid.*, p. 231.
11. *Haṭhayogapradīpikā*. *op. cit.*, II. 42.
12. *Ibid.*, II. 72, 73.
13. *Śrīś* Chandra Vasu, trans., *The Gheranda Saṁhitā*, ed. (London: Theosophical Publishing House Ltd, 1976), III, vv. 37-42.
14. A. Avalon, *The Serpent Power*, *op. cit.*, p. 209, n. 3.
15. *Ibid.*, *Ṣaṭ Cakra Nirūpaṇa*, p. 337.
16. *Ibid.*, p. 340.
17. *Ibid.*, p. 346.
18. *Ibid.*, *Serpent Power*, p. 47.
19. *Ibid.*, *Ṣaṭ Cakra Nirūpaṇa*, p. 349.
20. *Ibid.*, p. 372; it is also the praṇava, the mantra OṀ.
21. *Ibid.*, Commentary, p. 374.
22. *Ibid.*, *Serpent Power*, p. 126.
23. *Ibid.*, *Ṣaṭ Cakra Nirūpaṇa*, v. 35. Commentary, p. 403.
24. *Ibid.*, v. 37. p. 407.
25. *Ibid.*, p. 409, n. 6 by Avalon.
26. *Ibid.*, p. 412, v. 38, Commentary. The Brahmarandhra is the fissure in the skull whence the *prāṇa* escapes at death.
27. *Ibid.*, *Serpent Power*, p. 140; Woodroffe, *Garland of Letters*, *op. cit.*, pp. 182 ff. has a good account of the causal forms.
28. We have taken the list of seven from *Serpent Power*, pp. 140-143. As Woodroffe says, other Tantras list 6 to 12. See Woodroffe, *Garland of Letters*, *op. cit.*, pp. 180-184.
29. *Ibid.*, Woodroffe. *Garland of Letters*, p. 182.
30. *Ibid.*
31. Avalon. *The Serpent Power*, p. 143.
32. *Lalitā Sahasranāma*, *op. cit.*, quoted by Commentator, *Bhāskarāraya*, p. 60.
33. Avalon, *The Serpent Power*, *op. cit.*, p. 250.
34. *Ibid.*, p. 128. n. 2.
35. One day of the god Brahma's life is one *kalpa*; a *kalpa* is 4,320,000,000 years, at which time the worlds are dissolved. Then there is a period of the same length as the *kalpa* before the worlds are recreated. This is Brahma's

night. Three-hundred and sixty of such days and nights equals one year of Brahma's life. His lifetime is 100 of these years.

36. *Pāduka Pañcaka* (*Fivefold Footstool*), Commentary on v. 1, p. 482, *Serpent Power, op. cit.*
37. Sri Aurobindo, *On Yoga* : I : *The Synthesis of Yoga* (Pondicherry: Sri Aurobindo Ashram, 1955), p. 698.
38. Swami Muktananda, *Play of Consciousness, op. cit.*
39. Richard D. Mann, *The Light of Consciousness: Explorations in Transpersonal and Humanistic Psychology* (Albany : State University of New York, 1984). Professor Mann quotes profusely from Muktananda's account of his religious Tantric experiences.

VIII

TANTRIC VAIṢṆAVISM: SYMBOLS OF LIKENESS BETWEEN MACROCOSM AND MICROCOSM IN YOGA, MANTRA AND YANTRA

In our chapter title we did not use the word *identity* as the relationship between macrocosm and microcosm because Vaiṣṇavite Tantric thought, like Vaiṣṇava philosophy in general, belongs to the Hindu system of philosophy called Viśiṣṭadvaita (qualified non-dualism). In this school, Brahman is one (*advaita*), but is Saguṇa (with qualities) Brahman and not the Nirguṇa (without qualities or attributes) of the Advaita philosophical schools such as Advaita Vedānta and the Śaiva-Śakta. In Viśiṣṭadvaita God has the attributes of truth, goodness, beauty and bliss. He is the soul of matter and the soul of souls, but soul and matter are themselves ultimate realities like God, although dependent upon God alone who is the one independent reality. The relationship between God and the other two realities is like that between soul and body, an organic relationship. Thus man, though like God in having a soul that in its liberated state is essentially spirit and characterized by limitless knowledge is never identical with God, but remains an organic part of His being.

The ways to liberation in Tantric Vaiṣṇavism involve a rich symbolism integrally related to their metaphysical system which we shall briefly outline before going on to the ways of liberation through yoga, mantra and yantra.

Metaphysical System of the Pāñcarātra (Tantric Vaiṣṇavism. Brahman is all forms and yet no form "without beginning, middle or end."[1] From Brahman emanate the first personal form of

God. "best of *puruṣas*," with two arms, pure crystal in color and wearing a yellow garment. From Him emanates His *para* form described as four-armed and of a dark-blue color.[2] The Lord through Lakṣmī, His Śakti, creates and IS the entire cosmos of universes, all similar to our own.

The process of recreation after each *pralaya* (the dissolution state of the universes) begins when the Śakti of the Lord initiates another cycle of creation. Prior to this, She has been one with the *para* form of the Lord (called variously Viṣṇu, Vāsudeva, Narāyaṇa and other names in the Pāñcarātra texts). She begins creation like a lightning flash with Her dual activities of *krīya* (force) and *bhuti* (becoming).[3] This is the beginning of the first stage of Primary Creation or Pure Creation (*śuddhasṛṣṭi*) when the *guṇas* (attributes of the Lord as the highest personal god appear). This corresponds with the appearance of the Śuddha tattvas of the Śaiva-Śakta philosophy. The *guṇas* as attributes of the Lord are not the usual three of other Indian systems of philosophy which belong to *prakṛti*, but are designated *aprakṛti* (not belonging to *prakṛti*).

The guṇas of Vāsudeva number six: (1) *Jñana* (knowledge) here meaning omniscience; (2) *Aiśvarya* (sovereignty of the kind that is omnipotence); (3) *Śakti* (potency as power to become the material cause of the world; (4) *Bala* ((strength as power to sustain the entire creation; (5) *Vīrya* (virility interpreted mainly as immutability; (6) *Tejas* ("splendor, might" and also indicated absolute sovereignty and irresistibility[4]). These are also the attributes of Śakti. Sanjukta Gupta in his Introduction to his translation of *Lakṣmī* Tantra considers Lakṣmī the "Becoming or the subsistence of the absolutely existing God" and the "self-hood of the supreme self (*paramātman*), i.e. of God" and "His essential nature."[5] In addition Knowledge, first of the guṇas is Her essence as also the essence of Brahman.[6]

The six guṇas are the instruments of creation and issue forth as emanations in pairs called *vyūhas*. Each pair, however is Viṣṇu (and Lakṣmī) with all six guṇas of which two are exemplified in each pair. The *vyūhas* are named after members of Kṛṣṇa's family and are Saṁkarṣaṇa, Pradyumna and Aniruddha. To Saṁkarṣaṇa belong the guṇas *jñāna* and *bala*; to Pradyumna belong *aiśvarya* and *vīrya* and to Aniruddha *śakti* and *tejas*.

Saṁkarṣaṇa's function is superintending all individual souls and the separation of them from *prakṛti*. Pradyumna's province is the overseeing of the creation of human beings and their instruction in all sorts of religious observances. Aniruddha oversees the creation of the world and is its protector.

Next in the emanation process of creation are the Twelve Sub-Vyūhas. These play an important part in yantras and in the religious life of Vaiṣṇavite Hindus today who daily recite their names. They are grouped in threes, each group attached to one of the four *vyūhas* (Vāsudeva is also a *vyūha* and the first). From Vāsudeva come Keśava, represented as shining like gold and carrying four discusses; Nārāyaṇa, dark in color like the blue lotus, carrying four conchs; and Mādhva like a sapphire gem with four clubs.

The three sub-vyūhas descending from Saṁkarṣaṇa are Govinda, Viṣṇu and Madhusūdana. The three descending form Pradyumna are Trivikrama, Vāmana and Śrīdhara; and the three from Aniruddha are Hṛṣīkeśa. Padmanābha and Dāmodara.

These twelve sub-vyūhas are the deities of the twelve months of the year. Many texts add another set of twelve descending from the four Vyūhas. The additional twelve to make the twenty-four forms are derived by having Vāsudeva (who springs forth from the Vyūha Vāsudeva) give rise to Puruṣottama from whom comes forth Janārdana. Similarly the other two Vyūhas each emanate three. Thus we have the additional twelve to make the twenty-four forms.[7]

Also belonging to the first stage of primary or Pure Creation are the *avatāras*. These are the "incarnations of God or of his Vyūhas or Sub-Vyūhas of angels."[8] Schrader lists thirty-nine principal avatāras given in the *Ahirbudhnya Saṁhitā*, substantially the same as in the *Lakṣmī Tantra* and other Pāñcarātra *saṁhitās*. The list includes, except for Buddha, those most often mentioned in works on Hinduism: the Boar, the Fish, the Man-Lion, the Dwarf, Paraśurāma, Kṛṣṇa, Rāma and Kalkin.

The third kind of *avatāra* and the most important for yoga practice and meditation is the Antaryāmin. This is Aniruddha, the Antaryāmin (Inner Ruler) in all souls. He is like a "smokeless flame" in the "lotus of the heart" upon which the aspirant concentrates in yoga practice. However, another Pāñcarātra text, the *Padma Tantra*, places the Antaryāmin at a higher level than Aniruddha as the first emanation from the Divine, closer to the concept of the Antaryāmin of the Bṛhadāraṇyaka Upaniṣad.

Finally, as belonging to the first stage of the Pure Creation is Vaikuṇṭha, the Highest Heaven (*paravyoman*). This is located outside the Cosmic Egg (Brahmāṇḍa) whose upper regions merely contain temporal heavens. The Paravyoman is "infinite above, limited below."[9] Its transcendent nature is indicated by its name Tripād-Vibhūti "manifestation of three fourths" of God (*cf. Rig-Veda* (x. 90.4)). The Brahmāṇḍa manifests only one-fourth of the Divine. Vaikuṇṭha comes into existence with the Vyūhas and all its inhabitants, including Lakṣmī, at the dawn of a Kalpa and disappears with all its inhabitants at the Cosmic Dissolution at the end of a Kalpa. Another view, probably later, maintains that Vaikuṇṭha and all its inhabitants do not disappear at the Great Dissolutions, but are everlasting.

In Vaikuṇṭha there are both matter and spirit (souls). There is matter for there are delightful recreational facilities such as parks, lotus-tanks, pavilions, etc.; also God, the "angels," and liberated souls with bodies called *a-prākṛta* (non-natural). The matter essential for all these things and bodies is called *śuddha-sattva*. It is not the *sattva* guṇa nor any of the other guṇas or their combinations, but a kind of spiritual matter found only in the Pure Creation and described as "the nature of knowledge and bliss" and "nothing but wishes materialized."[10]

The central spiritual Being in Vaikuṇṭha is God Himself in His highest form and with his Śakti, Lakṣmī. God is resplendent with all the symbols that signify the entire cosmos, the macrocosm: (1) the *Kaustabha* Jewel worn on the breast which represents the souls of the universe; (2) the *Śrīvatsa* (a curl of hair on the breast) means Prakṛti (the matter of worlds); (3) a club equivalent to the evolute Mahat (intellect); (4) a conch shell signifying the sattvic Ahaṁkāra, another evolute; (5) a bow which is the Tamasic Ahaṁkāra; (6) a sword equated with knowledge; (7) its sheath symbolizing ignorance; (8) the discus that represents the tattva, Manas; (9) the arrows which signify the organs of perception and of action; and (10) the garland equated with the elements (probably the *tanmātras* and *bhūtas*). Altogether this gives us twenty-five tattvas that belong to man and the cosmos.

The souls inhabiting Vaikuṇṭha and enjoying the Vision of God are of two kinds: the Nityas (eternal ones) or Sūris (sages, masters) which correspond with the angels of Western religions, and the Liberated or Muktas. Both classes are endowed with omniscience, but the Nityas have always been free from defilement; also they hold certain offices and perform definite functions for God, though these duties are not made definite in the literature. In addition these angels are "door-keepers" and "town-watchmen" in God's city and make up the retinue of the deity. Three of the more famous angels either in the latter group or in addition to them are Ananta, the same as Śeṣa, the Serpent, who is Viṣṇu's couch; Garuḍa His well-known vehicle; and Viṣvakṣena, prime minister in both heavenly and earthly affairs.

The other and lower kind of inhabitants of this Highest Heaven are the Muktas. They are said to be of the nature of "intensely radiating spiritual atoms of the size of a *trasareṇu* (mote in sunbeam)."[11] Schrader points out[12] that this notion is based upon a passage in the *Mahābhārata* in the Śanti Parva which describes the journey to the Highest Heaven of the Liberated. It states that they pass through the door of Āditya (the sun) and "become consumed by his fire. They then become invisible, for after that they cannot be seen by anybody at any time."[13] In this state they are said to have entered into the Vyūhas, each by turn, and then finally into the Paramātmā, *Vāsudeva*. Schrader interprets this to mean that the souls are bodiless after having their subtle bodies burned up in their passage through the sun, though this means they merely have no karma-made body; they can assume a non-natural body or even several bodies simultaneously and travel anywhere in the universe. It seems unlikely that many of the souls would wish to engage in such activities because the Liberated are those whose only desire is closeness to God in Vaikuṇṭha. Here, they behold the form of God to which each devoted himself in his earthly existence; otherwise there is complete social equality. As in traditional Christain theology, the Vision of God is the everlasting bliss of the soul in Heaven.

With this account of Vaikuṭha we complete out account of the first stage of the pure or Primary Creation. The second stage begins with the Pure-Impure manifestations, the second stage of Primary Creation in which the *bhūti* (becoming) aspect of Śakti is active. First of the tattvas to appear are Puruṣa and Māyā Śakti. Puruṣa is, however, the Kūṭastha Puruṣa, an aggregate of souls like bees in a honeycomb, all impure because of their karma. This puruṣa is the totality and source of all souls bound by karma before the creation, and at the time of the Great Dissolution all souls return to him. He is a Pure-Impure tattva because he is in himself pure, but impure as container of the impure souls. He issues forth from Pradyumna, a Vyūha. To agree with the Puruṣa Sūkta of the *Rig-Veda*, the Kūṭastha gives rise to the four varṇas (Brahmin, Kṣatriya, Vaiśya, Śūdra) and subsequently to the Manus in pairs who are the ancestors of mankind.

Māyā Śakti is basically Mūlaprakṛti , the primordial "matter" of the universe. Pradyumna transfers both the Kūṭastha Puruṣa and Māyā Śakti to the Vyūha, Aniruddha, who through yoga develops them for a thousand years. Then from Aniruddha emerges Śakti, from Śakti, Niyati; from Niyati (restriction), Kāla (time); from Kāla the Sattva Guṇa; from the latter the Rajas Guṇa and from this the Tamas Guṇa. The three, Māyā Śakti, Niyati and Kāla correspond in function and meaning with the six kañcūkas of Śaiva-Śakta metaphysics where they are also among the pure-impure tattvas that limit the knowledge and powers of each being. The three guṇas that appear next are under the supervision of Aniruddha in the form of the Trimūrti; Viṣṇu, overseer of the sattva; Brahma of Rajas; and Rudra of Tamas. These deities with their Śaktis, respectively Lakṣmī, Sarasvatī and Gaurī are the powers underlying the formation of the uniform mass usually called Avyakta or Mūlapṛakṛti, primordial element of the universe. This is the guṇa-yoṇi (guṇa-womb) of the cosmos.

Then emerge all the rest of the tattvas beginning with Mahat (or Buddhi). These all belong to the *aśuddha* (impure), the Secondary Creation, and were listed above in our description of the ornaments and weapons of God in Vaikuṇṭha.With little difference they correspond with those listed in the chapter on Śaiva-Śakta metaphysics above.

Ways to Liberation

Here, the most pertinent to our theme are two forms of samādhi yoga: one a form of Kuṇḍalinī yoga, the other a form of Mantra yoga; and another discipline called Saṁyama yoga.

Kuṇḍalinī Yoga. As in the Śaiva-Śakta system of Kuṇḍalinī Yoga, there are six cakras called Lotuses, with different names. All the letters of the alphabet are contained on the petals of the six Lotuses with the same significance as in the Śaiva-Śakta metaphyics explained in the prvious chapters on Mantra and Kuṇḍalinī Yoga. In ascending the cakras, the yogin sheds all the tattvas of the Pāñcarātra philosophy, just as in the Śaiva-Śakta system.

The aspirant must visualize Śakti (Lakṣmī) as the "primeval absolute" that is within his body "extending flamelike" over all the Lotuses from the Anus to the Lotus between the eyebrows.[14] In meditating upon Her who is "absolute consciousness" he begins with the Anus lotus and proceeds upward through the rest of the Lotuses when "his mind becomes totally absorbed by (Śakti),"[15] a state called "Viṣṇu's absolute state." Presumably he identifies himself with Śakti (Lakṣmī) and with Her is one with Viṣṇu in His absolute state.

This process of Liberation, manifests all the aspects of the identity between macrocosm and microcosm already delineated in our chapter on Kuṇḍalinī Yoga, so need not be repeated here with the difference that the state of oneness with Lakṣmī may not be identity with the Ultimate Reality in its transcendent state, although there are passages in the *Lakṣmī Tantra* that make the nature of Lakṣmī close, if not identical, to that of Śakti in the Śaiva-Śakta system. In Chapter II of this Tantra, Brahman is said to be the "eternal 'I' " (*aham*) and "like a waveless ocean of nectar," is "concentrated consciousness," changeless and eternal, whose essence is "the experience of bliss."[16] Śakti is described as *ahaṁta*, the I-ness or I-hood of the Ultimate Reality, Vāsudeva. "Brahman is not differentiated from Śakti" in the absolute state when Brahman is like the "waveless ocean" with his six divine attributes fully manifested, and in the form of "concentrated consciousness, quiescent and not subject to expansion or contraction . . . "[17] Therefore this state is called non-dual (*advaita*).[18]

Lakṣmī, Herself, who is the divine teacher in the *Lakṣmī Tantra,* adds, "Realize that the relationship between me and the Lord is that of identity because without I-hood (i.e., without the essential quality of I) the I-entity would for want of association be meaningless."[19] Furthermore, "Knowledge is the primary expression of 'I' " and "absolute knowledge is the essence of Brahman Itself," also true of Śakti who affirms that Brahmans's and Her own state is "identical with knowledge."[20] The main argument here is that the relation between God and Śakti must be one of identity because the pure I without attributes (a nirguṇa Brahman) would be meaningless. Likewise, the attributes or "content" without the I (Absolute Knower) would be empty of significance.

Despite these passages affirming the identity of the two in the *Lakṣmī Tantra* and other Pāñcarātra texts, Schrader concludes that the two are "actually regarded as distinct" and that the dualism is "a makeshift for preserving the transcendent character of Viṣṇu. . . "[21] (This Viṣṇu is, of course, the Viṣṇu of Vaikuṇṭha, not the lower Viṣṇu, Preserver of the Universe as a member of the Trimūrti.) Schrader adds, that the transcendent character of Viṣṇu as Brahman is so much in the background in the Pāñcarātra literature that we only need be concerned with Lakṣmī who appears as the universe in the tattvas and is also the power who governs and who dissolves total creation at the end of the Kalpa.[22]

In the Liberation process, the yogin perceives his identity as microcosm composed of the tattvas with Lakṣmī as macrocosm, the universe composed of the tattvas. Like Śakti (Lakṣmī) at the Dissolution stage of the Kalpa, he rids himself of the tattvas through kuṇḍalinī yoga to be dissloved into Lakṣmī. In Liberation it is Lakṣmī whose grace bestows it; the soul is absorbed into Herself to become united with Viṣṇu. Yet, it seems that in this philosophy there is no postulate, no philosophical principle that the two are One in the relationship of identity in the transcendent state as there is in the Śaiva-Śakta systems. Liberation then, as absorption into Lakṣmī which is called "Viṣṇu's absolute state" may not be actual identity with Brahman, the Absolute Reality. Even Lakṣmī, as we noted above, is probably not meant to be identical with Brahman. Therefore, the state of the Liberated is no doubt one of eternal existence in the transcendental form described in our account above of Vaikuṇṭha.

Mantra Yoga. As in the Śaiva-Śakta philosophies, Mantra plays a very significant part in the ways to Liberation. Mantra is a way of Liberation in itself, if one of the supreme mantras is contemplated in all its manifold richness of meaning. Śakti, Herself, like the Śakti of the Śaiva-Śakta system is also the four states of sound: (1) Śantā, which is like the Parā state in the Śaiva-Śakta philosophy; (2) Paśyantī; (3) Madhya, like the Madhyamā; and (4) Vaikharī. (See Chapter II, Part II above for the definitions of these four states of sound.) We saw the importance of sound in Kuṇḍalinī Yoga, but the most significant sound-forms in Tantric thought are the great Mantras, which in themselves can give Liberation.

The *Lakṣmī Tantra* has a grading system for all mantras. Highest in rank are the Supreme Mantras which are correlated with the fourth stage of the soul's progress towards release, the Turīya state. An example of such a Supreme Mantra is the Tāraka. The Tāra or Tāraka Mantra is the celebrated mantra OṀ. Tāra is another name for Lakṣmī, but also the name of the famous consort of Avalokiteśvara, the great bodhisattva of Mahāyāna Buddhism. The name Tāra means "carrying across, a saviour, protector" and Tāraka "causing or enabling to pass or go over, carrying over, rescuing, liberating, saving."[23] Thus Tāra and Tāraka are appropriate names for Lakṣmī and her Supreme Mantra which have these functions. The goddess Tāra of Mahāyāna Buddhism has a similar function.[24]

The Tāraka Mantra is also called the Brahma-Tāraka because it is identical with Brahman. As we said, this is the mantra, OṀ. It is to be constructed with A+U+M and then adorned with Bindu and Nāda. The letter A represents Aniruddha, the letter U, Pradyumna, and the letter M Saṁkarṣaṇa, while the Bindu is Vāsudeva. The three Vyūhas have all the guṇas of Vāsudeva from whom they emanate. The integral unity and indivisibility of the four is the Nāda, and the "highest perfection of Nāda is the I-hood (of God) who is the highest goddess[25]," that is, Lakṣmī. She is also the "most subtle Śakti called the space that exists inside nāda."[26] Sanjukta Gupta, translator of this tantra, comments that space as used here "represents the supreme Brahman which is also the essence or soul of everything."[27]

The *Lakṣmī Tantra* then goes on to give the adept further details about the content of OṀ correlated with its three-and-one-half measure units. One unit is A, another U, another M, and the half-unit Nāda and Bindu. Lakṣmī, the narrator in this Tantra, informs us that any group of three found in this world is represented by the three letters of OṀ. For example, the threee fires *gārhatpatya* (symbol of the earth-world), *dakṣina* (symbol of the atmosphere-world) and the *āhvanīya* (symbol of the heaven-world); the three worlds of the Veda (earth, atmosphere and heaven); the three Vedas (Rig, Sāma and Yājur); the three *guṇas*; the three gods (the *trimūrti*); the three Vyūhas (see above); the three *varṇas* (the *śūdras* omitted) and the three basic vowels (a, i, u).

The group of three just listed are merely particulars based upon the basic phenomena of creation, the sun, moon and fire and all the tattvas from earth to the basic "matter" of the universe, *prakṛti.* From "a" all words have emanated; from"u" have come the sun, moon and fire; and from the "m" all the tattvas. The significance of the half-measure will be found in the following section after the *nyāsa* rite. OṀ is related to the states of consciousness of the Māṇḍūkya Upaniṣad.

After meditations upon the meanings of OṀ given above, which represent the Macrocosm including the tattvas of which he, as microcosm is composed, he takes the next step towards Liberation, Nyāsa. This is the placing of Nāda as the six divine *guṇas* or attributes of Vāsudeva. Each attribute is "placed" on the part of the body mentioned in the specific mantra for the part, and each mantra includes a particular vowel representing a particular one of the six divine guṇas. These mantras are : (1) *Oṁ aṁ hṛdāyaya namaḥ*, the heart mantra. The heart is touched as this mantra is uttered which centers upon the guṇa jñāna, represented by the letter "a" with bindu. (2) The head mantra is *Oṁ Īṁ śirase svāhā*. The head is touched as this mantra is uttered which centers upon the guṇa *aiśvarya* (lordship). (3) The third mantra is directed to the tuft of hair on the crown of the head which is touched and centers upon the guṇa Śakti (potency). (4) With the fourth mantra, which centers upon the guṇa, *bala* (strength), the shoulders are touched. (5) With the fifth which centers upon *vīrya* (immutability), the eyes are touched. (6) With the sixth mantra, concerned with *tejas* (might, splendor), the hands are touched because they wield the weapon, *astra*, which symbolically defends against vulnerability.

The *sādhaka* is now identified as microcosm with all six attributes (*guṇas*) of the highest consciousness, the Macrocosm. To make this more emphatic, the same guṇas are now placed symbolically with *upāṅga* (lesser, inferior) mantras on the minor parts of the body (navel, back, arms, thighs, knees and feet). The adept must now meditate "on the *Puruṣottama* existing in his own self," the microcosm.

The Puruṣottama (Supreme Person) of this, the *Lakṣmī Tantra*, has the same place in this work as the Kūṭastha of the *Ahirbudhnya Saṁhitā* who is also the "aggregate of souls" which the Puruṣottama is said to be. Like the Kūṭastha, the Puruṣottama receives into himself all karma-bound souls during the dissolution periods of the world cycles and sends them forth again during the creation periods. He is thus the Cosmic Jīva who includes all karma-bound jīvas, but who is himself in the Pure category of tattvas since he is untainted by karma.

The process of identification with the Cosmic Jīva is continued with steps that further such identification. The adept is to begin with the Viśva state of its existence, and end with its dissolution state as a separate entity. These states of existence or consciousness are the waking, dreaming, dreamless sleep, turīya and turyātīta. As in the Māṇḍūkya Upaniṣad these states are related to the mantra OṀ. The letter A of OṀ (A+U+M) is the waking state of which Viśva,. identified with Aniruddha, is Lord. In this state, material objects of the senses occupy the *jīva*. The adept must dissolve this state and its Lord in the Taijasa deity, Pradyumna, who is correlated with the letter U of OṀ and the dream state of existence or consciousness, a state that has greater reality because its objects are internal, more subtle as within the jīva's mind. Then this state is dissoved in the M of OṀ correlated with the deep sleep state called Lord Prajña in the form of Saṁkarṣaṇa. Since sense objects even in subtle mental forms disappear in this state, it is closer to the next into which it is dissolved, a still higher state called *turya* (or *turīya*) correlated with the half-measure of OṀ. This *turīya* state is a samādhi state of knowledge and bliss and has as its Lord Vāsudeva in whom knowledge abides, but this state merges into the next and the ultimate and final one, *turyātitā*, the ultimate state of Lakṣmī-Nārāyaṇa. The aspirant now merges himself into Lakṣmī "the divine I-hood (*ahaṁta*) belonging to Viṣṇu."[28]

This is the final step in the reintegration process wherein the adept as microcosm realizes his identity with the macrocosmic reality at all its levels and states of being. He has achieved this through comprehension of the meaning of the supreme mantra OṀ, through the *nyāsa* ritual of placing on the body the guṇas of the Divine Reality, through meditation on the states of existence of macrocosm and microcosm until the ultimate samādhi of the highest state, *turyātīta*[29] was experienced through Lakṣmī's grace. (Her grace is always necessary and She bestows it when the adept attains Englightenment.)

Saṁyama Yoga: the Nava-Padma-Maṇḍala. Saṁyama Yoga is a way of Liberation through ritual worship. An interesting example features the construction of the Nava-Padma-Maṇḍala similar in meaning and function to the Śrī Yantra of the Śakta. The way of liberation through worship in this maṇḍala involves three steps: (1) Bhutaśuddhi, purification of the body; (2) Images and process of mental sacrifice; and (3) External worship which involves construction of a cosmic maṇḍala.

(1) Bhūtaśuddhi. This is the process of involution whereby the aspirant dissolves all the tattvas and ultimately merges into Lakṣmī; then he evolves himself in bodily form again, but in a purified state. After this, *nyāsa* is performed by placing mantras on various parts of the body. Most significant are the mantras OṀ and *Hrīṁ*, both mantras of Lakṣmī, Supreme Śakti. These are placed all over the body from the crown of the head to the toes. The mantras merge into Lakṣmī, the "form of all mantras" and pervade the body of the devotee. The *Lakṣmī Tantra* declares that the yogin who, through this ritual and meditaion, acquires the knowledge that Lakṣmī and Viṣṇu are one and eternal "will never again be reborn.[30]" Whether or not he has attained this realization, through this ritual the aspirant is made pure in both body and spirit and ready for the rites of the Internal or Mental Sacrifice and of the External Sacrifice in which the cosmic maṇḍala is featured.

The purpose of the second step in this way of liberation called the *Internal or Mental Sacrifice* is to destroy "the impressions of the mind" arising from internal or mental objects. The devotee assumes the *padmāsana* or a similar posture to meditate. Then he divides the region of the body from *mūlādhāra* to the crown of the head into nine sections, each with its appropriate functions and meanings. The content of each of the nine is correlated with the parts of the gross and subtle bodies of the aspirant. In the *ādhāraśakti*[31] are the five gross elements which compose the gross body; the subtle body is represented by all the following eight sections in an ascending order: The *tanmatras*, the *karmendriyas*, the *jñānendriyas*, *manas*, *ahaṁkāra*; *buddhi*; *avyakta* (the primordial *prakṛti*) and the three guṇas (*sattva*, *rajas* and *tamas*).

This is a major step in the reintegration of the aspirant; he sees the identity between the tattvas in himself, the microcosm, with those of the macrocosm. After dissolving them as he ascends the nine sections as in *kuṇḍalinī* yoga, he goes on to identify himself with Brahman, the Absolute Reality as "the supreme intergral pair, Lakṣmī-

Nārāyaṇa. . (identical with) the All,"[32] but Brahman also "transcends the All," and is the "concentrated consciousness and bliss."[33]

Other rites are less relevant to our theme such as *pūja* rites performed to honor Lakṣmī, Nārāyaṇa and the unity of the two. Now that the yogin has been made pure by this process of mental sacrifice to destroy the impressions of the mind arising from mental objects, he is prepared to continue the process of reintegration and Liberation through the rites of the External Sacrifice, illustrated by the Nava-Padma-Maṇḍala.

The Nava-Padma Maṇḍala, a form of External Sacrifice. The External Sacrifie is performed to destroy the impressions caused by external objects. It is a sacrifice in which Lakṣmī is worshipped by external objects of enjoyment consecrated by Lakṣmī's gaze.

First a pavilion is built on the site seleced. Then in its center a platform is constructed and in the center of this a maṇḍala (the Nava-Padma-Maṇḍala) is drawn upon the floor. See Diagram IV of the entire maṇḍala.[34] In the center is a square occupied by nine lotuses which contain deities of great spiritual significance (see diagram). This maṇḍala of nine lotuses "contains the whole world and represents the exalted home of all the gods, which encompasses all (other) loci and is the paramount abode."[35] In other words, the maṇḍala symbolizes the entire macrocosm.

Directions are given for the worship of the deities of the nine lotuses after preliminary rites of consecration of the maṇḍala area and of food, water and flower offerings to the gods. Mantras accompany these rites. Then the adept invokes Lakṣmī existing in his heart and then the Supreme God, the "container" of Lakṣmī. He utters thrice the two mantras Tāraka (OṀ) as God's mantra form (also Lakṣmī's) and Tarika (Hrīṁ). The latter is another Supreme Mantra of Lakṣmī which symbolizes the deity's three forms as gross, subtle and absolute, or as the manifested universe at all its levels and the transcendent Brahman beyond.

Utterance of thee two mantras makes certain the presence of the deity. Then the yogin performs *prāṇayāma* while invoking the Supreme God in the twelve-petalled lotus of the heart (the Antaryāmin) to come forth. He comes forth like a flash of lightning and is envisaged by the devotee in the handful of flowers he is holding which are to be offered immediately to God on the spiritual seat, *bhāvāsana*, in the pericarp of

NAVA-PADMA-MAṆḌALA

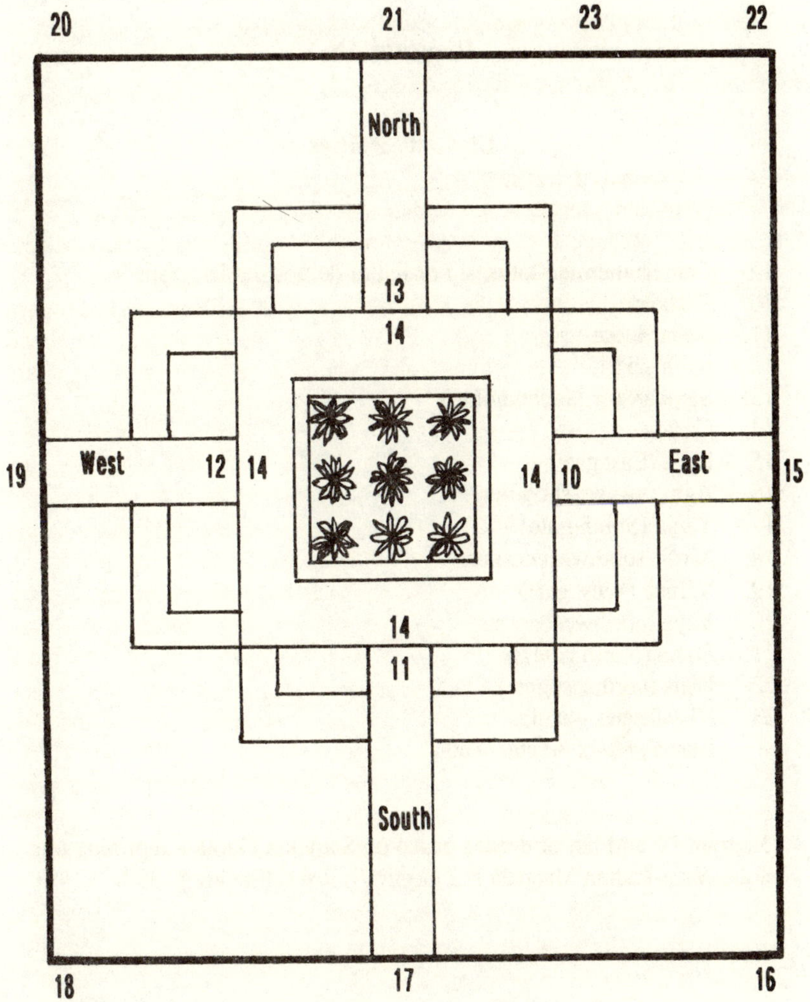

DIAGRAM IV

Diagram IV

List of Deities

1-9 Center: the nine lotuses. For list of deities see Diagram V.
10. Balākikā
11. Vanamālikā
12. Vibhīṣakā
13. Śaṁkarī (or Madhudīdhiti)
14. Garuḍa
15. Indra (East gate)
16. Agni (southeast corner)
17. Yāma (South gate)
18. Nirṛti (southwest corner)
19. Varuṇa (West gate)
20. Vāyu (northwest corner)
21. Soma (North gate)
22. Īśāna (northeast gate)
23. Viṣvakṣena—zenith
Bramā and/ or Anata—nadir

Diagram IV and list of deities based on Sanjukta Gupta's reproduction of the Nava-Padma Maṇḍala in *Lakṣmī Tantra* following p. 398.

THE NINE LOTUSES OF THE NAVA-PADMA-MAṆḌALA

DIAGRAM V

Diagram V

The Nine Lotuses of the Nava-Padma-Maṇḍala: List of Deities and Mantras

1. The Absolute Śakti (Lakṣmī) on Nārāyaṇa's knee.
2. Śikha (tuft of hair) mantra with conch shell
3. Māyā
4. Varma (armor) mantra
5. Jāya, with red disc
6. Lakṣmī (first emanation from Lakṣmī, the Absolute Śakti)
7. Śiras (head) mantra and goad mantra
8. Kīrti, lotus mantra on each petal of her lotus
9. Hṛdaya (heart) mantra, mantra of *vanamālā* on all petals

Meaning of Letters on Central Lotus

A. Lower half, Netra; upper half, Vāsudeva
B. Saṁkarṣaṇa
C. Pradyumna
D. Aniruddha
E. Lower half, Astra; upper half, Gulgulu
F. Lower half, Astra; upper half, Guruṇya
G. Lower half, Astra; upper half, Madana
H. Lower half, Astra; upper half, Śalala

Diagram V and list of deities and mantras based on Sanjukta Gupta's reproduction of the Nava-Padma-Maṇḍala in *Lakṣmī Tantra* following p. 398

the central lotus of the maṇḍala. The adept visualizes Viṣṇu as present "full of compassion and indulgence,"[36] and offers food, the bath, garments, etc, as in regular pūjāṣ. The absolute Śakti, Lakṣmī, is similarly worshipped. After this while reciting the mantra, Hrīṁ, he worships Lakṣmī as pervading the entire body of God. Then he invokes the great Goddess as "distinguishable"from the body of the Lord. She is "all-powerful, divine and unique" with a luminous body composed of the six Vyūhas and corresponds in all respects with the Lord's. Lakṣmī explains that she only accepted embodiment out of compassion for living beings to help them towards Liberation.[37]

Lakṣmī next instructs the aspirant in the placing of her retinue, that is, the deities emanating from Her, on the nine lotuses; but first, in the pericarp of the center lotus he envisages Her as the Absolute Śakti on the knee of Nārāyaṇa occupying the *bhāvāsana*, the seat of spiritual realization. Then he places Her main attributes personified as deities of Her retinue on the designated lotuses of the maṇḍala. (See diagram.)

The six mantras that represent the six divine guṇas or attributes of Vāsudeva, whose meanings have been given above, also have definite places on lotuses of the maṇḍala. They represent the main qualities of Vāsudeva as seen in Vaikuṇṭha by the Liberated.

After meditation upon Lakṣmī, Nārāyaṇa and the deities in Lakṣmī's retinue, the adept should meditate on the subtle form of the mantra Hrīṁ, the Tārikā; then on the mantra of the "Obsolute Tārā" who has the six attributes (the guṇas of Vāsudeva emanated in the Vyūhas) and "consists of consciousness." This is the "the divine absolute (state of) the couple. . . "[38] The yogin should worship Tārā[39] as the all-pervasive absolute in her forms of evolution and involution, i.e. as the total universe, then worship the absolute divine state of the couple mentally along with all the "objects of enjoyment" that are part of the ritual of worshipping the highest deities. Next the retinue of the couple is worshipped beginning with the four female doorkeepers of Lakṣmī, then Garuḍa and ending with Viṣvakṣena.

The following chapter of this Tantra describes all the "objects of enjoyment" to be offered in the worship. In the succeeding chapter the purpose of such ritual worship is made clear. It is the reintegration of the adept through identifying himself with Lakṣmī and Viṣṇu in his meditations on them and through the ritual actions related to the meditation.

Ultimately, when the aspirant feels the reality of the Divine Presence and oneness with It, he leaves the empirical world behind and "traverses the course beyond."[40] He "acquires identity with the category of "I,"'[41] which means oneness with Śakti since "I" (*aham*) is "the essence of God and of His Śakti."[42] Perhaps this means that the devotee is also one with Brahman.

But Schrader thinks that the general meaning and intent of such passages in Pāñcarātra texts that seem to express the *advaita* idea of identity of the ātman (individual soul) with the Brahman are not to be taken to mean identity. As an example he quotes a passage from the *Padma Tantra* that is a reply to the question asked of the Lord," What is the difference. . . between Thee and the liberated souls? "The Lord replies that "there is no difference whatever, " yet adds, "As I live. . . just so live the liberated souls."[43] This brings a plurality into the philosophy as in the Viśiṣṭadvaita school characteristic of Vaiṣṇava thought. It seems that if Schrader is right as in the Vaiṣṇava systems generally, the Pāñcarātra viewpoint holds that the liberated soul, though resembling God, is not absolutely identical with Him but lives a transcendental existence eternally in the presence of God in Vaikuṇṭha, the highest Heaven. If so, we do not have an identity between macrocosm and microcosm, but a close resemblance between the two and an organic spiritual relationship. God is the soul of souls and each soul a part (*aṁśa*) of God. Although the aspirant may realize this truth in each of the three ways delineated in the foregoing account-kuṇḍalinī yoga, mantra yoga or saṁyama yoga-according to the Lakṣmī Tantra it is saṁyama yoga which is "most pleasing to the Śakti."[44]

NOTES

1. F. Otto Schrader, *Introduction to the Pāñcarātra and the Ahirbudhnya Saṁhitā* (Madras : Adyar Library, 1916), p. 52p. n. 3.
2. *Ibid.*
3. *Ibid.*, p. 29.
4. *Lakṣmī Tantra*: A Pāñcarātra Text, trans. Sanjukta Gupta (Leiden: E.J. Brill, 1972), p. XXV and chap. IV. p. 21.
5. *Ibid.*
6. *Ibid.*
7. Schrader, *op. cit.*, p. 42.
8. *Ibid.*
9. *Ibid.*, p. 50.
10. *Ibid.*, p. 51.
11. *Ibid.*, p. 57.
12. *Ibid.* pp. 57 f.

13. *The Mahābhārata*, trans. Pratap Chandra Roy, sec. ed. 12 vols. (Calcutta: Oriental Publishing col, n.d.), Vol. X, sec. 345, p. 596. Schrader mistakenly says sec. 346.
14. *Lakṣmī Tantra, op. cit.*, p. 366.
15. *Ibid.*
16. *Ibid.*, p. 8.
17. *Ibid.*, pp. 8 f.
18. *Ibid.*, p. 9.
19. *Ibid.*
20. *Ibid.*, p. 10.
21. Schrader, *op. cit.*, p. 30.
22. *Ibid.*, p. 31.
23. Monier Williams, *Sanskrit-English Dictionary*, new ed., reprinted 1956-60 (Oxford University Press, 1899), pp. 443f.
24. D. C. Sircar, ed. *The Śakti Cult and Tārā* (Calcutta: University of Calcutta, 1967), "The Tārā of Candradvīpa" by D.C. Sircar, pp. 128-133. In This essay Sircar finds evidence that the deity, Tārā, origninated among aboriginal people of East India and "was adopted in both the Brahmanical and Buddhist pantheons in the early centuries of the Christian era."
25. *Lakṣmī Tantra, op. cit.*, p. 127.
26. *Ibid.*, pp. 127 f.
27. *Ibid.*, p. 127. n. 4.
28. *Ibid.*, p. 130.
29. *Ibid.*, p. 130, n. 3. Sanjukta Gupta explains that the "concept of turyātīta is peculiar to this system", and denotes the soul's "supra-Vyūha state of existence" in which its "divine majesty and splendour are fully manifested." I presume that this is its transcendental existence eternally in the presence of God in Vaikuṇṭha, the highest heaven.
30. *Ibid.*, p. 211.
31. Ādhāraśakti is Śakti in the Mūlādhāra and corresponds with the Kuṇḍalinī of the Śaktas also in the Mūlādhāra.
32. *Lakṣmī Tantra, op. cit.*, pp. 215 f.
33. *Ibid.*, p. 216.
34. There is a beautiful color diagram of this maṇḍala in Gupta's *Lakṣmī Tantra* Volume after which I have sketched mine.
35. *Lakṣmī Tantra, op. cit.*, p. 232.
36. *Ibid.*, p. 239.
37. *Ibid.*, p. 240.
38. *Ibid.*, p. 246.
39. Lakṣmī is called Tārā when worshipped as her mantra Tārikā.
40. *Ibid.*, pp. 266 f.
41. *Ibid.*, p. 267.
42. *Ibid.*, p. 267, n. 4.
43. Schrader, *op. cit.*, p. 91.
44. *Lakṣmī Tantra, op. cit.*, p. 86 and Introduction p. XXXII

PART III

SYMBOLS OF IDENTITY BETWEEN MACROCOSM AND MICROCOSM IN HINDU ART : PAINTING, SCULPTURE AND ARCHITECTURE

IX

A VIṢṆU MAṆḌALA FROM NEPAL

The Viṣṇu Maṇḍala we are about to discuss, painted in Nepal in 1686, is at present in the Prince of Wales Museum of Western India, Bombay, India. Its historical background is helpful in understanding its meaning. The Pāñcarātra cult of Vaiṣṇavism had become popular in Nepal by the fourth and fifth centuries A.D. Then, after the tenth century, Śaivism began growing and gaining ascendancy over Vaiṣṇavism. Buddhism, too, had entered Nepal by this time; thus varying degrees of syncretism of the three religions entered into the religious thought and practices of this Himalayan state. Hindu monarchs of the Thākuri and Malla dynasties often worshipped both Śaiva and Vaiṣṇava deities. The great king, Jayasthitimalla (1386-1429), though he also worshipped Śiva, was apparently a devotee of Viṣṇu as we know from the laudatory titles he used. One of these, Daityanārāyaṇāvatāra, actually calls the king an avatāra of Nārāyaṇa (Viṣṇu). This is, perhaps, the first instance we have of a Nepalese king naming himself an avatāra of the deity.[1] As Professor Pal notes, the Gurkha kings continued this practice and even today the king of Nepal is looked upon as an avatāra of Viṣṇu.[2]

In Nepal today there are still many Vaiṣṇava temples and images which are used for worship. The symbolism of the maṇḍala painting we are about to elucidate would no doubt be understood by some and appreciated by all of these Vaiṣṇava devotees. It is inclusive in its cosmic symbolism and a fine example of a Vaiṣṇava maṇḍala in the medium of painting. The occasion for the work was the celebration of the completion of the *anantavrata*, a popular rite in Nepal during the

VIṢṆU MAṆḌALA

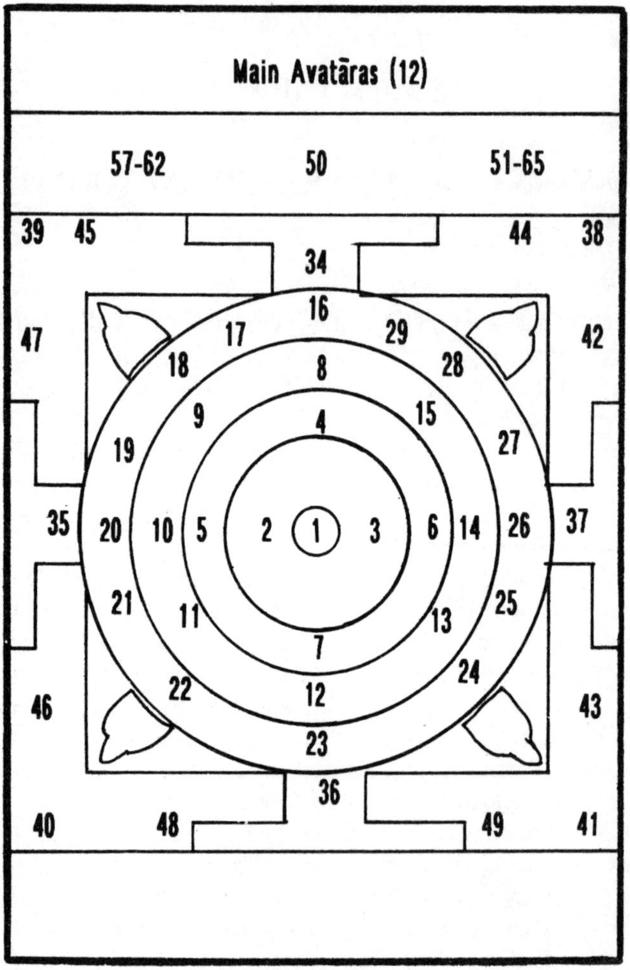

DIAGRAM VI

Diagram based on Pratapaditya Pal's photograph of this maṇḍala in the Prince of Wales Museum of Western India, Bombay, India. See Pal's *Vaiṣṇava Iconology in Nepal*, Fig. 16.

VIṢṆU MAṆḌALA

1. Vāsudeva
2. Lakṣmī
3. Garuḍa

4-7. The four Vyūhas

8-15. Subtle body of Vāsudeva (its eight components) or the eight nāgas.

16-29. Fourteen planes of the World Egg.

30. Ganeśa with Vedavyāsa
31. Viṣṇu
32. Mahākāla
33. Devī

34-37. The four principal Lokapālas

38-41. The lesser Lokapālas

42-49. Gateway guards

50. Viṣṇu in Sudarśana form

51-62. The twelve Subvyūhas

63-74. Twelve main *avatāras* of Viṣṇu

last few centuries, celebrated on the fourteenth day of the bright fortnight of the month of Bhadra.[3] Paintings such as this were consecrated on this day. The rite is centered upon the worship of Ananta, a name of Śeṣa, associated with Viṣṇu or his forms.

In the center of the maṇḍala (see diagram) is the white Vāsudeva in his Para form (four-armed and dark blue in color). Since it is the Para form of God that the Liberated see in Vaikuṇṭha, there is good reason to believe that the work as a whole is a representation of Vaikuṇṭha, the highest heaven of the Vaiṣṇavas.[4] Later, we shall find that it is even more, a representation of the entire cosmos, the Macrocosm.

Vāsudeva (1 on the diagram) is a standing figure flanked by two others. Lakṣmī on His right and Garuḍa (his vehicle) on His left. Lakṣmī has four arms and hands; one of the lower is in the teaching position, the other holds a lotus; one of the upper hands holds a vase, the other a manuscript. Garuḍa is six-armed.

In the second circle are four seated figures of Viṣṇu, each a different color: green, blue, yellow and white.

These are four *vyūhas* (4, 5, 6, 7) emanating from *para* Vāsudeva in the center circle and are : Vāsudeva, but a subordinate Vāsudeva who, according to some Pāñcarātra texts, emanates from the *para* Vāsudeva[5]: and the three usual *vyūhas* defined in the preceding chapter: Saṁkarṣaṇa. Pradyumna and Aniruddha.

In the third circle, there are eight male figures (8-15) of different complexions seated in yoga posture on a *nāga*. The hoods of the nāga extend behind each figure to form a canopy over his head. Each figure has his right hand in the posture of granting boons, while the left hand holds a lotus. These may represent the eight *nāgas*, the same as the Vasus who are attendants of Indra; or they may signify the eightfold subtle body of the deity called the Puryaṣṭaka[6] which means literally "the city of the group of eight," (the five *tanmātras, buddhi, ahaṁkāra* and *manas*) the tattvas which comprise the subtle body of the individual or the Deity. Or, the eight may represent the Kuṭastha Puruṣa in whom all non-liberated *jīvas* rest during *pralayas*, and from whom they go forth at the beginning of each recreation cycle; but here in relation to the number eight, he is made to fit into the Puruṣa of the Puruṣa Sūkta by saying that he consists of one couple from each of the four varṇas, the eight ancestors of the human race or the eight Manus. As such, he springs from the Vyūha, Pradyumna's mouth, arms, legs and feet.[7]

In the fourth circle, there are fourteen different forms of Viṣṇu (16-29). Each has a different color and holds the four symbols usually held by the deity; club, discuss, conch and lotus, but in different combinations.[8] Pal hypothesizes that these fourteen forms signify the fourteen planes of the cosmic World-egg produced from the navel of Padmanabha, a name of Aniruddha, whose function as Vyūha is the superintending of the recreation of the cosmos in each cycle. As Vyūha he is part of Viṣṇu, so Pal concludes that "the fourteen planes are segments of the Lord."[9] This means the entire cosmos, the Macrocosm, including the lower worlds beneath the earth and the lokas above the earth. This harmonizes with theViśiṣṭadvaita philosophy that conceives god as the soul of matter as well as the soul of souls.

Immediately outside the fourth circle and within the four corners of the square are four deities in arched shrines (30-33). These are Ganeṣa, Devī, Mahākāla and, Pal adds, "probably Viṣṇu."[10] At the four gateways are the principal Dikpālas (34-37), also called Lokapālas, the guards of these spatial regions, and in the corners are the other four Lokapālas (38-41) to guard these regions of space. There are guards also in a standing posture on each side of the four gateways (42-49); other figures in a sitting posture flanking both sides of each guardian may be *ṛṣis* and yogins, others *navagrahas* (planetary deities), and two are identified as Brahmā and Bhairava (a form of Siva) while the rest are probably *nityas* (eternal ones) and *sūris* (sages). These angels in addition to their official duties serve as town watchmen and door-keepers in Vaikuṇṭha.

At the very top of the panel-maṇḍala are the main avatāras of Viṣṇu (see diagram). Under this is a panel showing Viṣṇu (50) and His twelve sub-vyūhas on either side (51-56 and 57-62). Viṣṇu is shown standing on Garuḍa with eight arms which signifies his aspect as the Sudarśana Puruṣa. The ultimate meaning of this Puruṣa is brought out in Schrader's summary of the chapters of the *Ahirbudhnya Saṁhitā* on the power of the Sudarśana Mantra. Through this Mantra, Bṛhaspati obtains the vision of the Sudarśana Puruṣa who appears before him in a human form clad in a dazzling yellow robe. Bṛhaspati asks how this Puruṣa known as eight-armed can come before him in human two-armed form. The Sudarśana Puruṣa answers that he has four forms each with respectively two, eight, sixteen and sixty-two arms and a wondrous fifth form in which he appears as the All.[11] In another chapter of this Saṁhitā the Sudarśana is said to be "the Wheel of Time, the Highest Self the one who turns it and who appears as Brahmā, Viṣṇu, and Śiva at the times of creation, continuance, and dissolution of the world. . . "[12]. Thus all time is included in the maṇḍala as all space, the total Macrocosm. Viṣṇu is the All.

The significance and general meaning of this Viṣṇu maṇḍala is similar to that of the Śrī Yantra, although it lacks the fullness of detail of the latter. Like the Śrī Yantra, it is another beautiful example of a cosmic yantra whereby the adept can reintegrate himself with the universe at all levels, and ultimately with the Source of all, in Vaiṣṇava thought "that which has all forms and no form." The *para* form of God as Vāsudeva in the center of the painting reflects this Ultimate Reality, the Brahman. Lakṣmī, beside Him, his Mahāśakti, is His first primal link with the created worlds, one with Vāsudeva in Her absolute form; in her subtle and gross forms She is all the tattvas of the macrocosmic universe including, of course, all individuals. The aspirant's awareness of this is made explicit in the rites used in the worship of this maṇḍala. These are accompanied with significant mantras. Lakṣmī is to be worshipped with her mantra Hrīṁ, symbol of Her absolute, subtle and gross forms which include all levels of the macrocosmic universe and its Source. In comprehending this Mantra, the individual is made aware of his likeness as microcosm to Lakṣmī as Macrocosm. He knows he is composed of the same tattvas and has the same "forms," subtle and gross, and when Liberation is attained, resemblance to Lakṣmī in her transcendental absolute form, an eternal spiritual reality.

In addition to Lakṣmī there are other less significant links to the created universe, although the maṇḍala, itself, is a representation of the highest heaven, Vaikuṇṭha. These links are in the third and fourth circles. In the third circle, the eight male figures seated on *nāgas* may signify the subtle body of the deity *puryaṣṭaka*, the "group of eight" which also comprise the subtle body of the individual; or the eight may refer to the eight ancestors of the human race, the eight Manus. In the fourth circle, we may have the fourteen planes of existence of the Cosmic Egg produced from the navel of Padmanābha, a name of Aniruddha, who, as *vyūha*, is part of Viṣṇu. This makes the fourteen planes "segments of the Lord," Pal comments, and manifests the identity of God with the universe of individuals.

Space and Time are shown clearly in the painting: space in the Lokapālas, guardians of the regions of space (the entire Cosmos), and Time by Mahākala and by the Sudarśana Puruṣa's aspect as the Wheel of Time.

The adept, initiated into the meaning of this Cosmic Maṇḍala will find it a graphic aid in meditating upon the nature, meaning and Divine Source of all Being, and his place therein; and with his guru's help and Laksmī's grace, the ways that he, as microcosm may return to the Source, the Brahman in whom is also Lakṣmī. Some of the ways of return have already been treated in the chapter immediately above.

NOTES

1. Pratapaditya Pal, *Vaiṣṇava Iconography in Nepal* (Calcutta: Asiatic Society, 1970), p. 10.
2. *Ibid.*
3. *Ibid.*, p. 13.
4. *Ibid.*, p. 84 and see preceding chapter.
5. *Ibid.*, p. 83.
6. *Ibid.*, p. 84.
7. Schrader, *Introduction to the Pāñcarātra, op. cit.*, p. 61.
8. Pal, *op. cit.*, p. 82.
9. *Ibid.*, p. 84.
10. *Ibid.*, p. 83.
11. Schrader, *op. cit.*, p. 131.
12. *Ibid.*, p. 132.

X

KĀLĪ AND THE GARLAND OF LETTERS

Kālī as the great terrible manifestation of Mahādevī is a favorite picture found in homes of devotees and on the walls of shops in India. She is portrayed as black, nude and with a long garland of human heads around her neck; around her waist is a girdle of human arms severed at the elbow. In the hands of her four arms she is usually shown with one holding the head of a demon she has slain, another catches the blood of the demon in a bowl, the other two hands may each grasp a sword and a spear, or one may show the *mūdrā* of blessing and the other grasp a sword. She stands upon the inert body of Śiva. The locus of the scene is the cremation ground.

This terrible portrayal has the symbolism of a cosmic yantra whose central meaning is found in the garland of heads that Kālī wears. Our interpretation of this famous iconographic form is based upon the work of Sir John Woodroffe who reveals its full meaning.[1]

As we said, the Goddess stands in the midst of the burning or cremation ground (*śmaśāna*), a haunt of ascetics. The cremation ground symbolizes the death of the body and all its desires that keep the aspirant whirling about on the wheel of birth and death. That the Goddess is nude means that She is clothed in Space (*digaṁbarā*) or Unlimited. She is dark, symbolic of the Void, Nothingness, for She is Dissolver of the Universe into the Void; at the same time She is the All which is "Light and Peace."[2] The inert Śiva, upon whom She stands, is the *prakāśa* (illuminating) transcendental aspect of consciousness, the supreme *nirguṇa* Brahman, of which Kālī, Herself, is the changing, energy aspect. In Śakta and Śaivite metaphysics, as we have seen, the two are One.

The most fascinating element in such renditions of Kālī is the necklace of human heads that She wears as a garland. According to the Tantra-Śastra, this garland signifies the fifty (or according to some fifty-one) letters of the Sanskrit alphabet. We explained in Part II how Śabda (sound) and its meaning (*artha*) represent the entire universe.[3] Since the letters compose all the words (objects) and meanings, the Garland of Letters is the entire universe that Kālī creates, and as the Destroyer aspects of the Divine withdraws into Herself at the end of every world cycle.

The Tantric initiate, aware of the meaning of Śabda in Tantric philosophy, beholds in this necklace the entire Cosmos at all levels and its emanation-and-return cycles. Since we have already, as we said, treated the subject of Śabda and mantra at length in Part II, we need only summarize briefly the major aspects involved to show the relevant symbolism of Kālī's necklace.

Creation begins with the Causal Śabda, the Śabda Brahman, the dichotomy in Consciousness between the "I" and the "This," Subject and Object. In the Divine consciousness, it is the Cosmic Dreamless Sleep state (*suṣupti*) that corresponds with the same state in the individual, the microcosm. Then comes the stage in the cosmic creative process of the awakening in the divine Consciousness, when It "Ideated" or beholds the universe in idea-form. This is the Paśyanti-Śabda level of Sound. The Cosmic Mind then knows Itself as subject and object; as subject-cognizer it is Śabda and as object known it is subtle *artha*; it has not yet projected Itself upon the plane of matter. Śabda in this context is Madhyamā Śabda. Here are the letters, the Mātrikā or "Little Mothers" which are the subtle forms of the letters of gross speech.

Then the Cosmic Mind projects the subtle level of Śabda on to the material plane and has as *artha* the manifold physical objects of the universe. This is the Cosmic waking State (Jāgrat). Śabda is now Vaikharī-Śabda, thought expressed in speech through the physical body, the vocal chords. It is the letters of this speech that Kālī wears as a garland. In Part II we saw that these letters and names are objects, meanings and concepts of which the entire universe is composed. They *are* the Universe. Worn by Kālī as Destroyer, as severed human heads they signify the Dissolution of the Universe which they compose. Kālī withdraws the letters that are the Universe into Herself at the end of the Kalpa when all the levels of Śabda disappear. Then the dualism in Consciousness of subject-object relations vanish. There is neither "I" (Aham) nor "This" (Idam) but the one non-dual transcendent Consciousness of Śiva and Kālī merged into one.[4]

The Garland of Kālī functions as a symbol of Macrocosm and Microcosm to the Tantric devotee initiated into the philosophical meanings we have just summarized. The nature and meaning of the Cosmos in its Unmanifest non-dual aspect, and in its created aspect as the multiple world of the dichotomy of subject and object is portrayed in the letters of the Garland for those who know the meaning of Śabda and its non-dual Source. The fierce Destroyer aspect of Śakti, as Kālī, represented not only in the severed heads that are the letters, but in the severed human arms around her waist, and her holding of the severed head of a demon whose blood she catches in a bowl (and is said to drink)—all these horrible elements of the picture signify the transcience, the suffering, the unsatisfactoriness, despite its joys, of life in the birth-death world-cycles. The adept, aware of this, longs for the Dissolution symbolized by Kālī as Destroyer of the Garland of Letters. He does not need to wait until the end of the Kalpa when the universal Dissolution takes place. Kālī means to him the Dissolution also of the microcosm, of himself, of his individual gross and subtle bodies and the return to the One, Śiva-Śakti in non-dual union, the state of eternal Being, Consciousness and Bliss. The symbols of destruction of the Letters, the sword, the spear, the blood have this meaning. It is in this way that the pictures that show the Garland of Kālī function as symbols of the identity of Macrocosm and Microcosm for the aspirant seeking mokṣa.

NOTES

1. Woodroffe, *Garland of Letters, op. cit.*, pp. 193-217.
2. *Ibid.*, p. 213.
3. See Part II, chap. V, "The Cosmic Mantra: the Pāñcadasākṣarī Mantra," and Chapters VI and VII which also contain relevant materials.
4. Woodroffe, *Garland of Letters, op. cit.*, p. 216.

XI

THE TRIVIKRAMA FORM OF VIṢṆU

This celebrated form of Viṣṇu is represented in the impressive rock-cut relief sculpture *The Three Strides of Viṣṇu* (*Trivikrama Viṣṇu*) at Mamallapuram (near Madras), which was executed about the middle of the seventh century. The theme of the three strides of Viṣṇu is an ancient one that begins in the *Rig-Veda*.[1]

As the noted Indologist F.B.J. Kuiper comments, most scholars of our time identify the three steps of Viṣṇu either with the course of the sun, its rising, its culmination at noon and its setting, or with the three divisions of the Vedic universe, earth, atmosphere and Heaven.[2] Kuiper, however, relates the three strides to a creation myth of the *Rig-Veda* in which Indra plays the leading role. Viṣṇu and Indra together participate in the creation of the universe. Kuiper points out that whereas Indra was protagonist of the Devas only, Viṣṇu could represent their antagonists, the Asuras, also. Viṣṇu's relation to both groups is shown in his two vehicles, Garuḍa the Suparṇa, the glorious bird and sky-dweller and Śeṣa, the serpent of the subterranean waters in the nether world. Thus Viṣṇu had a place in both worlds and therefore was able to represent "the unity of the two antagonistic parties, upper world and nether world,"[3] i.e., the Devas and the Asuras. Thus his position was that of the Center. He is given the position of *dhruvā dik* (the Center as the nadir), in the later *Atharva Veda* and other Vedic literature.

In Kuiper's view, Viṣṇu's place in the creation myth is this: Before Indra's work of creation there was only "the beginning of the primordial hill." Indra opens the hill and raises up the sky. In this context Viṣṇu strides forth. His first step is the nether world, his second the upper world, but the third is a mystery not visible to the eye because it represents the totatlity of both worlds, their synthesis.[4]

Later Hindu literature, e.g. the Śanti Parvan of the *Mahābhārata* and the Purāṇas relate the three strides to the myth of the Vāmana *avatāra* of Viṣṇu. For devotees, the third step is perhaps the most significant, since it reaches and includes the heaven-world as the other two include earth and atmosphere. Earlier than the *Mahābhārata* are references to the three strides of Viṣṇu in the *Śatapatha Brāhmaṇa* which also interprets them as including earth, atmosphere and heaven. In Chapter II of Part I above we noted that these steps were emulated by the king in the Rājasūya rite with the same significance.[5]

To return to Kuiper's interpretation of the Vedic story, it is important to note that he relates the three strides to the Skambha, the Cosmic Pillar, whose meaning we discussed in some detail in Part I above.[6] The Cosmic Pillar is grounded in the nether world like the *dhruvā dik* and ascends to Heaven. Viṣṇu during the creation "rose up from the center . . . so he is connected with the pillar which now supports the sky," and "is the connecting link which forms part of both "worlds."[7]

As Kuiper notes, later art represents Viṣṇu arising from Mt. Meru as the cosmic pillar, a notion that harmonizes with either Kuiper's interpretation of the Vedic myth or the later story of the Vāmana *avatāra*. A monumental representation of *The Three Strides of Viṣṇu* showing him also as the Cosmic Pillar is reproduced in The *Art of India* by Stella Kramrisch.[8] It is a rock-cut relief in Varāha cave II at Mamallapuram executed in the seventh century. Professor Kramrisch, in her commentary on this work, describes its form and meaning. Its height is about five feet, eight inches. The right foot of the deity rests in the lower world of the vanquished demons; the left foot has progressed through the air-world marked by figures of the Sun, Moon and a mid-air dweller; the toe of Visnu's left foot, raised very high, is being worshipped by Brahmā in the highest of heavenly abodes (except for Vaikuṇṭha, paradise of the Liberated). Dr. Kramrisch adds that Viṣṇu is represented also as the Cosmic Pillar, support of the universe. This is plain in the sculpture; the right leg is strongly braced in a straight line with the torso.

This is an eight-armed form of the deity. The weapons he carries are the bow, shield and conch on the left; the sword, club and discus on the right. The weapons and ornaments in their symbolic meaning reveal "in what manner Viṣṇu bears the whole world, abiding in his nature."[9] The *Viṣṇu Purāṇa* in its interpretation of the meaning of the weapons and ornaments became the standard one for subsequent literature including the Pāñcarātra works. (In Part II, Chapter VIII,

"Tantric Vaiṣṇavism" an account has been given of the symbolic meanings of all the weapons and ornaments). Their general meaning is to show that He is indeed the Cosmos as Macrocosm. He is all the tattvas, all the constituents of the universe in their gross and subtle manifestations. The Lord is Time and beyond Time; His "form is all worlds"; His shape is all visible things; yet "without shape or form,"[10] i.e., transcendent. Assuming the form of sound He is the Vedas and "religious manuals, poems, and all that is said or sung."[11]

After this identification of Viṣṇu with all aspects of the Cosmos, the Macrocosm, and as the Ultimate transcendent Brahman beyond, the Purāṇa adds, "The man who knows these truths shall never again experience the afflictions of worldly existence."[12] This means that knowing and meditating upon the form of Viṣṇu as the Cosmos, the Macrocosm, functions to reintegrate the aspirant and liberate him from the *saṁsāra*. He is now able to find himself in the vast universe, the Macrocosm, and above all he realizes that he, as Microcosm is one with It in all its aspects, both the material, physical changing and the unchanging or eternal. He knows that this highest consciousness, the Knower, the Ātman, is the eternal self within him and that it is one with, in the sense of a part of, the transcendent eternal Soul of the Lord.

The noble rock-cut relief sculpture of *The Three Strides of Viṣṇu* at Mamallapuram is a vivid representation of Viṣṇu as the world-axis, the Cosmic Pillar, the Center and Support of the Universe. In addition, the weapons and ornaments that to the adept signify all the tattvas and all the souls of the universe as parts of the body and soul of the lord, mean that He is the universe itself, the Macrocosm. Meditation upon this identity between the Lord as Macrocosm and himself as microcosm, functions to reintegrate the aspirant so that with Lakṣmī's grace "he shall never again experience the afflictions of worldly existence."

NOTES

1. *Hymns of the Rig-Veda*, trans. Ralph Griffith, 2 vols., Chowkhamba Sanskrit Studies, Vol. XXXV (Chowkhamba Sanskrit Series Office, 1963), Vol. I, Book I, 154, p. 207.
2. F.B.J. Kuiper, "The Three Srides of Viṣṇu," in *Indological Studies in Honor of W. Norman Brown*, ed. Ernest Bender, American Oriental Society Seires, Vol. 47 (New Haven: American Oriental Society, 1962), PP. 137-157.
3. *Ibid.*, p. 144.
4. *Ibid.*, p. 549.

5. See the sections on the Vājapeya and Rājsūya rites for a full account of the relevance of the Viṣṇu strides to the notion of the Cosmic Axis, Center of the Universe, Part I, Chapter II of this book.
6. *Ibid.*
7. Kuiper, *op. cit.*, p. 150.
8. Stella Kramrisch, *The Art of India* (London : Phaidon Press, 1955), Plate 85, description p. 206.
9. *ViṣṇuPurāṇa*, trans. H.H. Wilson, 3d ed. (Calcutta: Punthi Pustak, 1961), Book I, chap. XXII, p. 129
10. *Ibid.*, p. 130.
11. *Ibid.*
12. *Ibid.*

XII

MACROCOSM AND MICROCOSM IN THE ŚIVA NAṬARĀJA

A great school of sculpture called the Southern School of Indian Bronzes flourished between the tenth and thirteenth centuries. Among the best as works of art and of religio-philosophical significance which can be seen today in art museums in India and elsewhere in the world, are the dancing Śivas, Śiva Naṭarājas. Among the very best are the *Naṭarāja* from Kankoduttavanitam (South India) in the Government Museum, Madras, India,[1] and another bronze of the eleventh century *Śiva, Naṭarāja Lord of Chidambaram* in the Rijksmuseum, Asia Department, Amsterdam.

There are, however, figures of Naṭarāja everywhere in South India. Most important and famous for Śaivites is the *Chit Sabha* at Chidambaram in Tamilnadu, which is in the center of the temple compound.

From early times Śaivas have held Chidambaram to be a very sacred place; by the seventh century it was already famous.[2] Chola rulers covered the *sabhā* with gold; rebuilt in the tenth century, it has again today been covered with gold.[3] Famous Śaiva saints and scholars lived and wrote there to add to its glory.

Chidambaram is also called Puṇḍarīkapuram (Lotus-City) because it is considered to be the lotus-shaped heart of Virāt, the collective gross body of the cosmos which corresponds with that of the individual.[4] Far above and beyond this, it is the spiritual center of the Universe, for it is in this sacred space that Śiva dances, the place where the human meets the Divine. At the same time, this Center is said to be in the human heart of man, the microcosm. More will be added later about the religio-philosophical interpretation of the dance.

To return to the Sabhā which is the locus of the Dance, there are stone steps significantly five in number plated with silver leading into the Chit Sabhā. These five steps represent the five syllables of the Śaiva Pañcākṣara (five-syllabled) Mantra: Namaḥ Śivaya.[5] Inside the Chit Sabhā we behold Śiva Naṭarāja; on a separate pedestal at his left is Śakti in her aspect as Śivakāmasundarī. On Śiva's right is the Chidambaram Rahasya without any *liṅga* or image; instead there is simply a *tiruvāśi*, an arch with a veil in front. There is nothing behind the veil but empty space, symbolizing the formless, infinite, invisible Reality. This formless form is, however, also meant to be the *ākāśa* (ether) *liṅga*, one of the five *liṅgas* in India each representing one of the five elements ; ether, water, fire, air and earth.

This, then, is the setting for the celebrated Śiva Naṭarāja in the Chit Sabhā of Chidambaram. The Naṭarāja here, like all the authentic bronzes depicting the Dance of the Lord, has the following characteristics: Śiva is shown with four hands, and in a dancing posture with one leg raised. His hair is braided in yoga fashion and jeweled; in the violence of the dance the braids fly out at the sides of his head but are neatly stylized in horizontal symmetrical rows of braids. In his hair are a cobra, a grinning skull, a figure of Gaṅgā (personification of the Ganges River), a wreath of Cassia leaves, and the crescent moon. He is adorned with necklaces, armlets, bracelets, anklets and rings. He wears tight short pants of tiger skin which end between the thigh and knee, a jeweled belt and the sacred thread. A loose scarf flutters gracefully about and away from his body. The upper right hands holds a small drum, the other is raised in the *abhāya* (fearlessness) *mudrā*. In the upper left hand is a flame, the lower is extended towards the left foot which is raised. The right foot stands firmly upon the *asura*, Muyalaka. The figure of Śiva with Muyalaka below is on a lotus pedestal base whence emanates on either side an arch ringed with flames that encircles the entire dancing figure. In some works the arch is almost a circle, in others in the shape of a horseshes arch called the Tiruvāśi.

In its general meaning, the Dance represents the five cosmic activities of the Lord: (1) *Sṛṣṭi*, creation and evolution; (2) *Sthiti*, preservation and support; (3) *Saṁhāra*, destruction and involution; (4) *Tirobhāva*, veiling, illusion and giving rest; (5) *Anugraha*, grace, salvation, *mokṣa*.

ŚIVA NAṬARĀJA

DIAGRAM VII

Creation is symbolized by the drum with its rhythmic beating. We saw, especially in the chapters above on Tantric thought both Śaiva-Śakta and Vaiṣṇava, that *nāda*, followed by the Śabda Brahman (OṀ) , i.e., vibratory phenomena, are the first movements in Creation of the universe. This resembles the Big-Bang modern theory of the beginning of our Universe which also posits something like vibratory phenomena at the beginning when atoms were in their formative stages. Śiva's drum, therefore, is still an appropriate symbol of creation.

Another creation symbol is the serpent in the Lord's hair,[6] sign of the cosmic force called Kuṇḍalinī, central in the way of reintegration called Kuṇḍalinī Yoga described above in Part II. Kuṇḍalinī in her journey from Sahasrāra to Mūlādhāra represents the evolution of the universe; her upward journey from Mūlādhāra to Sahasrāra the involutionary return journey to the non-dual Brahman. Śiva, who is the archetypal yogin, wears the serpent as the sign of this cosmic coiled power of creation, preservation and destruction or involution. Another creation symbol lies in the meaning of the sacred thread which the deity wears since its strands signify the tattvas of which the universe is composed.

Other creation symbols are the male-female aspects of Nature and the Oneness (non-dual union of Śiva and Śakti) represented by the Lord's earrings, a male earring on one ear, a female on the other. In this context we should remind ourselves that one of Śiva's names is *Ardhanārīśvara* (the Lord who is half-female, and male.) Finally, the goddess Gaṅgā in His hair is another fertility symbol and thus related to His creative powers since she is the personification of the Ganges River. Śiva, himself, brought her to earth from the heavens and benevolently let her flow through His tresses least the guishing waters injure Earth and her creatures.

All these creative functions, symbolized by the drum, the serpent, the sacred thread and the male-female earrings are dramatically summarized by a Tamil poet in these words: "Our Lord is the Dancer, who, like the heat latent in firewood diffused His power in mind and matter, and makes them dance in their turn."[7] This theory of the universe, though poetically expressed, is close to contemporary notions of the nature of the material world. Fritjof Capra in his book *The Tao of Physics* has a chapter with the title "The Cosmic Dance" prefaced with a dancing Śiva drawn in dynamic dots, lines and spaces that represent subatomic interactions between particles and "forces." He writes that subatomic physics demonstrated that the world of matter is a dynamic one with ceaseless interactions "manifesting itself as the exchange of particles; a dynamic interplay in which particles are created and destroyed without end in a continual cosmic dance of energy."[8]

The main symbol of Preservation in the sculpture is the raised right hand in the gesture of the Do-not-fear *(abhāya) mudrā*. The devotee who knows that the Lord is creator and controller of all Nature, the entire cosmos, has an overall fearlessness. Though he may suffer dire tribulations, he knows that ultimately, if he makes sufficient effort in this, and if necessary, in his next lives he can become one with the Lord, the ultimate goal.

Other symbols of Preservation are the coiled Kuṇḍalinī, sign of the Lord's immense Power; the ongoing creativity of the deity in the male-female earrings representing the continuing fertility, the continuance of the world of nature; the goddess, Gaṅgā has a similar meaning. Another symbol of the Lord's concern for the universe is the necklace of *rudrākṣa* beads interpreted by His devotees as solidified tears wept by Him for their sufferings.[9] The sacred thread is a Preservation as well as a Creation symbol because its many strands signify, as we said, all the tattvas which are the constituent elements of the entire Cosmos.

The major symbols of Destruction and Involution are the flame in the upper left hand of Naṭarāja and the *prabhamaṇḍala*, flames like a halo all around the *tiruvāśi* (arch). Other important representations of destruction and involution at the macrocosmic level refer to the cosmic dissolutions, the destruction of each recreated universe at the end of kalpa of 4,320,000,000 years. Then the world remains in dissolution for an equal length of time, the *pralaya*, before it is again recreated. There has been no beginning and there will be no end to these cycles of creation and dissolution.

Not only does Śiva's dance resemble the continuous incessant movement of the constituents of the physical universe, its repetition forever kalpa after kalpa poetically expresses what may be another truth about our cosmos. Carl Sagan observes that "the most elegant and sublime" of the Chola bronzes of the eleventh century is the representation of "the cosmic dance of Śiva."[10] These works, he comments, are "a kind of premonition of modern astronomical ideas."[11] Then he goes on to explain that the commonly accepted Big-Bang theory of the origin of the cosmos does not inform us about the final end of this vast universe. One hypothesis about the end, is based upon the theory that the universe, apparently expanding from the time of its origin, will continue to do so until the elementary particles as "a thin cold haze" will be all that is left.[12] The other hypothesis is like the Indian, a cyclical one, the theory that if there is more matter in the universe than we have yet observed perhaps "hidden away in black holes, say, or in hot but invisible gas between the galaxies—then the universe will hold together gravitationally and partake of a very Indian succession of cycles. . .Cosmos without end."[13]

The ashes on Śiva's body (remains of corpses at the burning grounds) and the skull remind the aspirant of the inevitable end of all living creatures in each rebirth of their existence in the world cycles. From the microcosmic point of view, and in relation to the reintegration, the involution of the individual phenomenal self as mind and body, the ashes and skull signify their annihilation so that the *ātman* can realize its identity with, and be absorbed into the Brahman, the Ultimate Reality, Source of all Being.

The major symbol of *tirobhāva* (veiling, illusion, *māyā*, *avidyā*) is the dwarf-asura, Muyalaka, upon whom Śiva's right foot is standing. This means to the adept, that Śiva destroys māyā, i.e., the mistaking of the phenomenal world and self for the Real. When this veil of illusion is destroyed, the aspirant may know and become one with the Ultimate Reality. He will know the All in the One and One in the All, the perennial truth discovered by all great mystics.

Anugraha (release, grace) is represented by the left lower hand which is pointed towards the raised foot. This gesture expresses the Lord's concern for his devotees, especially for those whose hearts and minds are intensely and entirely concentrated upon oneness with the one Self, Śiva as the non-dual Brahman. By His grace, he aids them in experiencing oneness with Himself, thus releasing them forever from bondage to the birth-death cycles. The process of release is the process of reintegration of the adept.

Macro-microcosmic Symbolism and the Reintegration of the Aspirant. In the Naṭarāja sculpture we have already noted many of the macro-microcosmic relationships that are potent aids in reintegration. We shall now summarize them. First there is the identity between the tattvas which are the mental, vital and physical components of macrocosm and microcosm. The *Mahimnastāva*, an ode in praise of Śiva, and one of Hinduism's most revered religious poems says of Śiva: You are the sun, you are the moon, you are wind, you are fire, you are water, you are space, you are the earth. . . we know not that element here which you are not."[14] The total material universe is, in fact, represented by the Sacred Thread the deity wears, since its many strands signify all the tattvas of which the universe is composed.

Space and Time are manifested respectively by the four arms as the four regions of Space, and by the Three Eyes which symbolize

Present, Past and Future. Their significance as Sun, Moon and Fire is another reference to Time. The Moon as one of the deity's eyes and the Crescent Moon on His head refer to time periods, the Moon to the monthly and the Sun to the yearly. In addition to their being Time symbols, Moon and Sun are names given to two of the most important *nāḍīs* in Kuṇḍalinī Yoga, Īḍā and Piṅgalā, another correspondence betwen macrocosm and microcosm. We have already noted above, that fire as a time symbol signifies both the time span of the macrocosm, the Cosmos, which is the kalpa in recurrent cycles, and the birth-death cycles of the individual, the microcosm. The skull the Lord wears on his head and the ashes smeared on His body have meanings similar to Fire, but fire, ashes and skull have a still more profound spiritual meaning. They signify the burning up of the ego, the *ahaṁkāra*, with all its appendages leaving the devotee only the *ātman* which is one with the ultimately real Self, Śiva as the Brahman.

The adept now aware of all these identities between macrocosm and microcosm, is prepared to meditate upon the eternal spiritual symbols present in the Naṭarāja which lead to identity with the Lord. Śiva is, himself, the archetypal yogin, the meaning of the serpent in His hair. Also, as we said, the serpent represents Kuṇḍalinī, the coiled power of Śakti utilized in Kuṇḍalinī yoga. The yogin knows that the cakras of this yoga within himself as microcosm also have macrocosmic existence in the body of Śakti as described, for example, in the *Saundaryalaharī* (see Part II, Chap. VII above) and also a more mundane existence geographically in six cities of India called the Six Ādhāra Sthalas.[15] The Mūlādhāra Sthala is in Tiruvarur, Svādhiṣṭhāna in Tiruvanaikovil, Maṇipūra in Tiruvannamalai, Anāhata in Chidambaram, Viśuddha in Kalahasthi, and Ājñā in Kaśi (Varanasi).

Mantra, too, is deemed significant to the yogin meditating upon the Dance of the Lord. The *Unmai Vilakkam*, verses 33-35 relates the five-syllabled (*pañcākṣara*) mantra of Śiva (Śi-vā-ya-nā-ma) to His dance thus:

"In His feet is *nā*; in His navel is *ma*;
In His shoulders is Śi; in His face *vā*;
In His head is *ya*."[16]

This text then declares that if the mantra "be meditated upon, the soul will reach the land where there is neither light nor darkness and Śakti will make it one with Śiva."[17]

The mantra OṀ, very important in both Śaiva-Śakta and Vaiṣṇava Tantric philosophies as we have seen in Part II above, also is related to the Cosmic Dance of Śiva in the *Unmai Vilakkam* where the arch is said to be the hook of the written symbol and the rest the "contained splendor,"[18] but a more adequate and more philosophical interpretation of the mantra OṀ in relation to the Naṭarāja is found in the Tamil work the *Tiru-Aril-Payan*, ch. IX.3.[19] Here the arch represents the dance of Nature (the Śakti of Śiva); the dancing Śiva within it the Dance of Wisdom. The yogin seeking Liberation is told: "The Dance of Nature proceeds on one side; the Dance of Enlightenment on the other . Fix your mind in the center of the latter."[20] Coomaraswamy offers a philosophical commentary on this passage given to him by Mr. Nallasvami Pillai.[21] He interprets the Dance of Nature as the dance of Matter, of energy in all its forms and symbolized by the arch; it is OM (*omkāra*) and the Dance of Kālī. The Dance of Śiva within the arch is the *akṣara*, another part of OṀ which is the *ardhamātra* (half-measure), the *nāda* and *bindu* written thus in Sanskrit ँ. This *ardhamātra*, Mr. Pillai says, is the fourth letter of OṀ. The three letters are A, U, M, (the O of OṀ is a diphthong A+U). Thus OṀ has four letters written thus in Sanskrit: ॐ.

The fourth letter of OṀ, as early as the *Māndūkya Upaniṣad*[22], is said to signify the fourth state of existence, *caturtha* or *turīya*, the state of oneness with the Ultimate Reality, the Brahman. It is because it is this state, the goal of the yogin, that the *Tiru-Aril-Payan* advises him to concentrate on Śiva's Dance of Enlightenment to attain *mokṣa*.

The yogin who comprehends and contemplates upon the many rich symbolic meanings of the Dance of Śiva perceives the identities between macrocosm and himself as microcosm in both their material and spiritual aspects. In this way, the Dance of Śiva is a potent aid in the reintegration of the aspirant. The mantras OṀ and Śivāyanāma are further aids. Contemplation upon this wealth of symbolism is eminently conducive to spiritual self-realization. This comes when, with the help of a guru for guidance perhaps in the method of Kuṇḍalinī Yoga, the devotee is able to shed all the tattvas of the world of māyā, of Kālī. Then he may experience oneness with Śiva-Śakti as the non-dual Brahman, thus attaining liberation.

NOTES

1. T.A Gopinatha Rao, *Elements of Hindu Iconography*, 2d ed., 2 vols. (Delhi: Motilal Banarsidass, 1968), Vol II. Part I, see photograph, Plate LVI facing p. 252, for the bronze in the Government Museum, Madras, India; see Herman Goetz, *The Art of India*, 2d ed. (New York: Greystone Press, 1964), p. 154 for a photograph of the work in the Amsterdam Museum.

2. Rao, *ibid.*, p. 229.
3. *Ibid.*, p. 230.
4. B. Natarājan, *The City of the Cosmic Dance* (New Delhi: Orient Longman Ltd., 1974), p. 3.
5. J.M. Somasundaram Pillai, *The University's Environs: Cultural and Historical*, A Silver Jubilee Souvenir of the Annamalai University, 4th impression, rev. and enlarged (Annamalainagar : Annamalai University, 1963), p. 70.
6. *Ibid.*, p. 84, footnote.
7. Coomaraswamy, Ananda, "The Dance of Śiva," in Rao, *op. cit.*, p. 238. Rao quotes the entire essay by Coomaraswamy. The book of essays entitled *The Dance of Śiva* (Bombay: Asia Publishing House, 1948 reprinted 1952), has the same essay but omits part of it and does not use the Sanskrit terms for some of the words.
8. Fritjof Capra, *The Tao of Physics*, paper ed. (Boulder, Colorado: Shambhala Publications, Inc. 1975), p. 225.
9. Pillai. *op. cit.*, p. 84, footnote.
10. Carl Sagan, *Cosmos* (New York: Random House, 1980), p. 259.
11. *Ibid.*
12. *Ibid.*
13. *Ibid.*
14. W. Norman Brown, *The Mahimnastāva* (Poona, India; American Institute of Indian Studies, Publication No. 1, 1965), p. 17.
15. Natarajan, *op. cit.*, p. 89.
16. *Ibid.*, p. 87.
17. *Ibid.*
18. Coomaraswamy, *op. cit.*, p. 92.
19. *Ibid.*, pp. 92f.
20. *Ibid.*, p. 92.
21. *Ibid.*, p.93.
22. See Part I, ch. 3 below.

XIII

MACROCOSM AND MICROCOSM IN THE HINDU TEMPLE

The Hindu temple is a manifest form of the Divine Reality as the Macrocosm in microcosmic form. Its function is to aid in the reintegration of the adept who meditates upon it as well as a place of worship. All temples are "the house, body and substance for God (the essence) to dwell in,"[1] so have the relevant symbolic form. We shall rely upon the great and well-known work *The Hindu Temple* by Professor Kramrisch for the symbolic meanings of the temple in relation to macro-microcosmic identities.

First in all temples is the underlying plan, the Vāstupuruṣamaṇḍala, the groundwork of the edifice. It is a ritual diagram that does not necessarily coincide with the site of the sacred precincts; it may be the site of the temple building only or merely drawn upon the altar. It is always of definite form, the dominant ones composed of either 64 or 81 squares. It is drawn upon the ground prior to the building of the temple, and upon it the temple stands actually or symbolically.

Vāstu in the name Vāstupuruṣamaṇḍala means the site, the place where bodily existence will be given to the Puruṣa. The Puruṣa refers to the divine Person whence Existence originates (see the Puruṣa Sūkta, *Rig-Veda* X. 90 mentioned in Part I, Chapter I). Maṇḍala in the name refers to the ritual diagram upon which the entire temple structure is founded.

Since the entire space-time cosmos at all levels is symbolically represented, it requires the knowledge of a learned Brahmin to guide the building of the structure from the Vāstupuruṣamaṇḍala to its completion. The Brahmin guides the architect (*sthapati*). The patron of the building is the *yajamāna* (sacrificer) who supplies the financial means, and like the *yajamāna* of the ancient Fire-Altar ritual receives the ultimate in spiritual reward through being identified with the Puruṣa in body and spirit as it is given manifestation in the temple. Beyond this, the temple has the more universal function of serving as a monumental visual aid in the reintegration of aspirants through meditation upon its meaning. The pilgrim usually does this by the rite of circumbulation (*pradakṣina*). In this rite he may, at the highest level, identify himself as microcosm with the Macrocosm symbolized in the temple, a potent aid in his spiritual journey towards reintegration.

The Vāstupuruṣamaṇḍala, the diagrammatic ground plan of the structure, portrays symbolically the macrocosm and is in the shape of the squares.[2] It may contain a variety in the number of squares within it, but there are two predominant forms; the maṇḍala of 64 squares called the Maṇḍūka, and that of 81 squares called the Paramaśāyika. The Maṇḍūka adequately represents the "hierarchy of ordered existence" in the tabular form without the image of the Vāstupuruṣa. The Paramaśāyika also represents the image of the Vāstupuruṣa, and whereas in the Maṇḍūka some of the deities can occupy only half a square, each deity occupies a complete square in the Paramaśāyika. The number of squares in each of these maṇḍalas is significant. In the Maṇḍūka, the number 64 is 8 x 8 which represents the celestial order derived from its source the Eight Suns with their rulers, the Ādityas. (The notion of Eight Suns is based upon the view that the sun enters one by one each of the eight quarters of space from sunrise to sunrise). The number 81 of the Paramaśāyika is 9 x 9 and nine is significantly 3 x3. Three refers to Agni's threefold state, his manifestations on earth, the air-world and the sky; but he has three fires in each of these regions, a total of 9.[3]

These nine forms of Agni refer to the macrocosm; corresponding with these in man, the microcosm, are the nine immanent breaths (*prāṇa*). The Paramaśāyika maṇḍala represents the subtle body of the Vāstupuruṣa with its "parts, limbs and apertures" co-terminous with the diagram of 81 squares whereas the Maṇḍūka of 64 presents the entire universe in its hierarchical order without coinciding as precisely with the image of the Vāstupuruṣa.[4] Both are adequate symbols of the Mahāpuruṣa as the Universe, an emanation from the Center (Brahman).

The size of the Vāstupuruṣamaṇḍala is not significant. It may be as large as the building site, or the temple, or of a standard minimum area. All the lines that divide the maṇḍala into smaller squares and the diagonal lines drawn within the enclosure have a definite width. "The archetypal measure" of the width is called Prāṇa, "immanent Breath or Energy (pneuma),"[5] the immortal part of the body. With this network of Prāṇa lines, the body of the Vāstupuruṣa endures as long as the present kalpa.[6]

The points of intersection of the Prāṇa lines are the "vital parts and tender spots (*marma*)" of the Vāstupuruṣa, so extreme care must be taken not to place heavy objects or building parts such as walls, pillars, beams, or windows on these places. Another very important reason for avoiding injury to these places is the identification of the *yajamāna* with the Vāstupuruṣa. If certain *marmas* suffer interference, the Vāstupuruṣa as organism is thrown out of order; the Yajamāna correspondingly suffers ill health; and if the vital parts of the Vāstupuruṣa are affected such as the head or heart of the maṇḍala, the Yajamāna may die.

The Yajamāna has this more personal magical relationship with the Vāstupuruṣa, but for all men the Puruṣa is the equivalence of man and the Universe, the Macrocosm.[7] The Puruṣa is the representative man in whom the Brahman is beheld. Although Brahman transcends space, time and form, It is comprehended intuitively by man as being within himself as microcosm and within the universe, the Macrocosm. Thus the maṇḍala is a device that binds the Brahman within its limits, and in its plan depicts the hierarchy of Its manifestations. The Puruṣa of the Vāstupuruṣamaṇḍala like the Primeval Puruṣa of the Puruṣa Sūkta "is this entire world past and future," and at its center, the Bramasthana, shines forth the light of Brahman.[8]

Dr. Kramrisch shows how the puruṣa of the Vāstupuruṣa maṇḍala has its prototype and origin in the Fire-Altar ritual. We saw that in this rite, the Yajamāna is identified with Agni-Prajāpati in the performance of this sacrifice. The golden man in the altar is the Yajamāna who becomes the Puruṣa as Macrocosm in the Fire-Altar built up as a replica of the space-time universe, the Macrocosm. The same symbolism is continued in the Vāstupuruṣamaṇḍala. The Vāstupuruṣa is the Agni-Prajāpati of the Fire-Altar, but drawn in man's likeness with the head in the East in the maṇḍala of 64 squares, the legs opposite, etc.[9]

The original "disintegration," the dismemberment of the Puruṣa to form the world described in the Puruṣa Sūkta is looked upon as a fall from the Brahman and coming to earth.[10] The fall from Brahman, the one, is represented as a pride-swollen Asura who falls with his face down "buried in the soil, part of it."[11] In this state, the buildings set upon him have a firm foundation. Thus the Asura as foundation and protector of the building is named Vāstupuruṣa, puruṣa of the site

(Vāstu). He is thought of in this way in the installation rites of the temple.

But the devotee who worships the Vāstupuruṣa beholds him "in his true state, facing upwards whence he had fallen."[12] He is now in the same position as the reconstituted Agni-Prajāpati of the Fire-Altar with gods on his body. In this state, he affords the foundation for an ascent to the higher regions and ultimately to Brahman by means of the temple structure built upon his body.[13]

There is further interesting macro-microcosmic symbolism, in the correspondence between the fallen Asura (the macrocosm) who is at first formless and nameless and man, the microcosm. The fallen Asura sinks down as ugly and powerless, lifeless and identity lost; but the gods descend upon him, become his body, and he is given form and name. The *Mahānirvāṇa Tantra*, in its description of a similar situation, declares that in man, the microcosm, when all the tattvas have been dissolved through yoga, a black man is visualized in the "left cavity of his abdomen, the embodiment of all sin. He is the size of a thumb, with red beard and red eyes, holding a sword and shield, angry, with his head ever held low."[14] Then a description is given of the rites that enable the adept to rid himself of the evil black man. When these are performed he receives "a new-born Deva body,"[15] just as the Asura receives his new Deva body when the gods descend upon him. The Asura now receives the name "Vāstu." "*Its image is that of the Puruṣa, the place of reference in which man beholds the identity of macrocosm and microcosm.*"[16]

The gods descend in a total of forty-five deities to give the Asura his new Deva body. They are his limbs and vital parts. Brahmā, the creator-god, is in the center called the Brahmasthāna which covers an area of four squares in the Paramaśāyika plan. In both plans, twelve gods form the inner rim of twelve squares and thirty-two gods the outer rim.

First, there is Brahmā in the center in the Brahmasthāna, which radiates the light of Brahman represented by Brahma. This deity occupies the area from the heart to the belly of the Vāstupuruṣa. This region, the Brahmasthāna, is the vital center of the Vāstupuruṣa as organism. Here are the Mahāmarmas, the most tender spots. Dr. Kramrisch likens this place to the Brahmapura in the individual as microcosm. Brahmapura means "city of God," and is mentioned in the Chāndogya Upaniṣad 8.1.1.6. In his commentary on this Upaniṣad, the philosopher, Śaṅkara, interprets the meaning of Brahmapura as the body of man in which the "lotus-flower" mentioned in the Upaniṣad as within the Brahmapura, is the heart, and in the heart or lotus-flower says the

Upaniṣad, is the entire universe with Brahman as its eternal Center. At the Macrocosmic level, Dr. Kramrisch comments, "the place of Brahman (Brahmasthāna) corresponding to Brahmapura in the universe is Hiraṇyagarbha. . . the primordial germ of cosmic light."[17]

From the Brahmasthāna, as from the cosmic light of the Hiraṇyagarbha at the dawn of creation, issue the twelve suns, the Ādityas. They occupy the inner rim of the squares, twelve in number. Since their Vedic number is only eight, only eight appear in the diagram, but four are named in pairs in the corners, while the other four each occupy a full side of the inner rim to make twelve. One of the four in pairs, Mahīdhara, also known as Pṛthivīdhara, is significant in a special way. Pṛthivīdhara means literally "earth-supporting" and refers to Viṣṇu as Ananta, support of the universe.[18] In like manner, the Vāstupuruṣa upholds the earth on which the temple is built. In tantric thought, Viṣṇu is the Regent of the world below and Brahmā Regent of the world above. In the diagram, the vertical axis of the temple symbolically rises from the "below," i.e., from Pṛthivīdhara, the Ananta of the Macrocosm, to the "above," the heavenly world symbolized by Brahmā who looks upward to his Source, Brahman.[19] Especially for the Tantric yogin, this is another example of the symbolic identity between macrocosm and microcosm since the world axis corresponds with the suṣumnā in the individual, the microcosm, that leads upward to the Sahasrāra where oneness with the Ultimate Reality is experienced.

The regions of the outer rim of the temple plan represent the entire space-time universe, the entire macrocosm and man's journey through it towards final salvation, union with the One, Brahman. He begins with the Celestial Region of the East, continues through the South where he beholds the world of the ancestors, abode of Yama, King of the Dead. Then he goes on to the dark world of the West where he meets such figures as Manu, the law-giver and prototype of man, and Rahu, symbol of Time or Duration, and the gods who personify the ills of man in this world such as Pāpayakṣman, Consumption, and Soṣa, Emaciation and Withering-up. Finally, he reaches the hopeful region of the North which lies between the dark West and bright East.

To summarize, the Vāstupuruṣamaṇḍala radiates from its Center, the celestial effulgence of the dark creative Light of the Brahmasthāna. First come forth the twelve Ādityas who take their places in the inner rim. Then, in the outer rim, thirty-two Nakṣatras take their positions. The functional meaning of the deities in their regional places is to include all aspects of the space-time universe, celestial and terrestrial. The total number of deities that comprise the maṇḍala as the body of the

Vāstupuruṣa is forty-five. If we take the number of deities in the outer rim, thirty-two, and add Brahmā (who stands for Brahman) at the Center, we have the Vedic number thirty-three that represents the gods. Although the thirty-three gods we have described are not the same as those of the *Rig-Veda,* they, too, like those of the *Rig-Veda* are inclusive of the significant aspects of the "three worlds" earth, atmosphere and heaven. The thirty-three gods occupy the "center and periphery" of the body of the Vāstupuruṣa.[20]

For the sacrificer, the Vāstupuruṣamaṇḍala has the form and function of building up a "ritual divine body in which the transcendent Center is Brahman.[21] The ritual body built up is a microcosm, a replica of the Macrocosm of Existence in the three worlds which radiates from the divine Center. Not only the sacrificer, but the initiated devotee who knows the macro-microcosmic symbolism of the Vāstupuruṣamaṇḍala and of the temple built upon its plan, identifies himself with it in his body (the universe of existence) and with what is beyond, that to which the Brahmā at the Center points, Brahman the Ultimate Reality. For him, the meaning of the Vāstupuruṣamaṇḍala and of the entire superstructure is Brahmāsmi (I am Brahman).

The Temple Superstructure. This is basically a mountain and cavern; it is symbolically the substantial body or form of the Mahāpuruṣa of the Puruṣa Sūkta. As both mountain and puruṣa, it is the form appropriate for communication between Heaven and Earth. (In other cultures, notably the Mesopotamian—cf. the Ziggurat—the mountain has been the form for the temple as means for this same communication.) The "mountain" is the tower, superstructure or *śikhara* of the temple and represents Mt. Meru, the axis of the universe in mythical Purāṇic geography. Spiritually and symbolically, however, which is the significant aspect of Mt. Meru, this axis of the universe is the upward path of the ascent for the human soul, the suṣumnā of the Tantric yoga described in Part II above. It is also the path downward of the divine toward the human, to draw the soul of man upward. In both these paths, the deity infuses the entire superstructure as well as the ground-plan, the Vāstupuruṣamaṇḍala.

The Garbhagṛha, the "cavern" in the mountain corresponds with the "cave in the heart" in the individual, the microcosm, the place of God-consciousness. The Garbhagṛha is square in plan and utterly dark; it is the abode of the essence of God. An image or symbol may represent the deity, but the wise see the Garbhagṛha as Hiraṇyagarbha, the Golden Germ, whence all the universe is derived.[22] The darkness is a super-luminous one, a blinding effulgence that irradiates the universe and gives rise to the myriads of forms.

The door of the Garbhagṛha usually has an image of the divinity in the interior over its center. On the center of the threshold of the entrance, is a lotus which is the symbol of the universe; no one may step on this. On the sides of the door, the river goddesses most often *Gaṅgā* and *Yamunā* are sculptured.

The towering edifice over the Garbhagṛha, the *śikhara*, has three main parts which probably signify the three regions of the universe according to the Vedas: earth, atmosphere and heaven. The earth-world is represented by the plinth or foundation at the bottom of the structure and often has a terrace for circumambulation. However, whether or not such a terrace is provided, circumambulation (*pradakṣina*) is performed by devotees who visit the temple for the primary purpose for which it was built, *darśana*, insight or direct vision of the religious reality symbolized by the complete structure.

The middle region of the *śikhara* represents the atmospheric region of the macrocosm. It is profusely decorated with many sculptures, but the most conspicuous are the large sculptures in niches or "windows" (*gavākṣas*). In each is depicted an aspect of the divinity of the temple. The massive curvilinear pointed-arched outline of the wondow-like niches are adorned at the apex of the arch with the "Face of Glory," the *Kīrttimukha*. It is known also as the *simha-mukha* (lion's face) and has the mien of a lion with horns, bulging eyes and chinless. It is a symbol of Time, the Devourer.[23] As the dragon of solar power, emitting fiery breath, it is also the Puruṣa, and because of its Lion's look and breath it is the Supreme Spirit, according to Professor Kramrisch.[24]

Of the other temple sculptures, the most significant belong to a type which abounds on all Indian temples whether Hindu, Jaina or Buddhist. These can be classified as images of Śakti and of reintegration. The lion-like animal, the *Śardūla*, is interpreted as "the Lordly Power of the wild beasts, who is Prakṛti, Śakti, Māyā."[25] Its function in the life of the contemplator is related to the life of action (karma yoga); he who is qualified can confront and ride the Śardūla. The Śardūla is also Śakti as Vāc (Śabda) whence comes the created universe (see the section on Vāc in Part I, Chapter I).

For aid in the development of the more contemplative natures not suited for "riding the Śardūla" there are the various images of Śakti as celestial beauty which Dr. Kramrisch interprets as signifying "embodied intellect."[26] The sculptor shows them as atmospheric bodies of prāṇa and movement, not as physical bodies of flesh and blood.[27]

Another theme prevalent on Indian temples is *maithuna* which for the initiated has the symbolic meaning of "reintegration." The couples in dalliance represent the reunion, the reintegration of the soul with the Divine. Such erotic imagery is common in Tantric literature.

Having in *darśana* perceived the meanings in these spheres of the temple-puruṣa, the philosophical aspirant is now prepared to ascend to the highest regions of the spirit, the "*sahasrāra*" of the structure. The door to this third world, the Heaven region, is the *Āmalaka*, a disc-shaped stone with ribs around the edges probably representing the sun-disc. It is likened to the pericarp of the sky-lotus, analogous to the thousand-petalled lotus of the Sahasrāra door to the Unmanifested, the Formless spiritual world of the One in Tantric yoga.

Having now passed beyond the door (*Āmalaka*) to the eternal world beyond, represented by the Kalāśa and finial of the temple, the adept reaches the point-tip of the finial which signifies the experience of unity with the One, the Supreme Spirit, goal of the arduous spiritual journey.

Summary of Macro-microcosmic Symbolism in the Hindu Temple. The Vāstupuruṣa of the Vāstupuruṣamaṇḍala, the ground-plan of the building, is the Mahāpuruṣa analogous to the Agni-Prajāpati of the Vedic Fire-Altar. As in the Fire-Altar rite, the yajamāna identifies himself as microcosm with the Mahāpuruṣa which represents the pattern of the macrocosm that includes all the regions of Space with their contents and all Time including the *kalpas*. The Brahmasthāna in the Center, points the yogin to the Ultimate Reality, just as in the microcosm the god-consciousnesss in man's "center" the heart, is source of man's desire for oneness with the Divine.

In the superstructure of the temple, the Garbhagṛha, the Golden Germ (Hiraṇyagarbha) is the base of the central axis directly over the Brahmasthāna (symbolically, if not actually). F.D.K. Bosch calls the Hiraṇyagarbha "the germ and womb of all that lives . . . and it is filled with the golden elixir of life."[28] This golden elixir is *amṛta*, the nectar of immortality, another symbol of the aspirant's quest. From the Golden Germ rises the entire macrocosm, the universe with its central axis, symbol of the *axis mundi*, the Mt. Meru of the temple. In the individual, the microcosm, the corresponding "axis" is the Suṣumnā of Tantric yoga. In the macrocosm, this axis rises from earth through the atmospheric heavens to the Āmalaka, then piercing it, becomes the finial that symbolically goes beyond the space-time worlds after passing through heavenly lokas. At the point-tip of the finial is, symbolically, the One, Brahman. In the individual, the microcosm, a similar journey is experienced in Tantric yoga, in the ascent from the Mūlādhāra whose tattva is "earth" through the hierarchy of the lower and higher heavens to the Sahasrāra which corresponds with the Āmalaka of the temple to culminate in the experience which pierces or transcends all time categories to attain oneness with the non-dual Brahman. This ascent of the cakras is analogous to the similar spiritual journey up to the finial of the temple that symbolically pierces into the eternal realm.

Whether or not he has practised Kuṇḍalinī Yoga, the devotee initiated into the meaning of the plan (the Vāstupuruṣamaṇḍala) and superstructure of the Hindu temple can, in Pradakṣina, meditate upon its significance as a monumental symbol which, as representation of the macrocosmic universe, manifests all the aspects of man's the microcosm's, situation and ultimate destiny, i.e., oneness with the Ultimate Reality.

NOTES

1. Stella Kramrisch, *The Hindu Temple*, 2 Vols. (Calcutta: University of Calcutta Press, 1946), Vol. I, p. 6.
2. The square shape in Indian thought is the perfect form because it represents Earth as the reflection of the heavenly world. The square is derived from the cardinal points, North, South, East and West. East and West have sacred significance because the Sun rises in the East and sets in in the West, with North and South the corresponding intermediate points. (See Kramrisch, *The Hindu Temple*, Vol. I, p. 17.)
3. Kramrisch. *op. cit.*, pp. 42. f. These nine are: three forms on earth: Sarva (water), Parjanya (rain), and Paśupati (plants); three in the atmosphere: Vāyu or ugra (air), Rudra, the storm-wind, and Aśani, the lightning; two in the sky-world: Mahādeva, the Moon, and Īśāna, the Sun; and the ninth form is Kumāra (the boy). *Ibid.*, p. 49, n. 83. Kramrisch cites as her source *Ś.B.* VI. 1.3.18.
4. *Ibid.*, p. 49.
5. *Ibid*, p. 51.
6. *Ibid.*
7. *Ibid*, p. 67.
8. *Ibid.*
9. *Ibid.*, p. 71.
10. *Ibid*, p. 73.
11. *Ibid*, p. 78.
12. *Ibid.*
13. *Ibid.*

14. *The Great Liberation* (*Mahānirvāṇ Tantra*), trans. and Commentary by Arthur Avalon, 4th ed., (Madras: Ganesh & Co., Private Ltd., 1963), vv. 98-99. Dr. Kramrisch refers to this passage which I have quoted.
15. *Ibid.*, vv. 100-103.
16. Kramrisch, *op. cit.*, p. 84, my italics.
17. *Ibid.* p. 89.
18. *Ibid.* p. 90, n. 86.
19. *Ibid.*
20. *Ibid.*, p. 94.
21. *Ibid.* pp. 95 f. and p. 96, n. 109.
22. *Ibid.*, pp. 164 f.
23. *Ibid.* p. 328.
24. *Ibid.*
25. *Ibid.* p. 337.
26. *Ibid.*, p. 340.
27. *Ibid.*
28. F.D.K. Bosch, *The Golden Germ* (The Hague: Mouton & Co., S'-Gravanhage, 1960), pp. 62-64.

BIBLIOGRAPHY

Agrawala, Vasudeva S. *Chakra-Dhvaja*; The Wheel Flag of India. Varanasi: Prithivi Prakashan. 1964.

Agrawala, Vasudeva S. *Śiva Mahādeva*: The Great God. Varanasi: Veda Academy, 1966.

Auboyer, Jeannine. *Le Trône et son Symbolisme Dans L'Inde Ancienne*. Paris: Presses Universitaire de France, 1949.

Basham, A.L. *The Wonder That was India*. New York: Macmillan. 1954; New York: Grove Press, paper ed. n. d.

Beal, Samuel, trans. *Life of Hiuen-Tsiang* by the Shamans Hwui Li and Yen Tsung. 2d ed. London, 1911. Reprint, Westport, Conn.: Hyperion Press. 1973.

Bhattacharji, Sukumari. *The Indian Theogony*. Cambridge: University Press, 1970.

Bhāskararāya (Śrī Bhāskararāya Makhin). *Varivasyā-Rahasya* and its Commentary. Trans. and ed. S. Subrahmanya Sastri. 3d ed. Madras: Adyar Library and Research Centre, 1968.

Bosch, F.D.K. *The Golden Germ*. The Hague: Mouton & Co., 1960.

Brown, W. Norman. "The Sources and Nature of Puruṣa in the Puruṣa Sūkta." *Journal of the American Oriental Society* 51:108-118.

Brown, W. Norman. "Agni, Sun Sacrifice and Vāc: A Sacerdotal Ode by Dirghatamas (Rig Veda L. 164)." *Journal of the American Oriental Society* 88: 199-218.

Brown, W. Norman. "Theories of Creation in the Rig Veda." *Journal of the American Oriental Society* 85: 23-24.

Brown, Norman. "The Creative Role of the Goddess Vāc in the *Rig-Veda*." *Mahfil*. Vol. VII, Nos. 3 and 4, 1971, 19-27.

Brown, W. Norman, Trans. and ed. *Saundaryalaharī*. Cambridge: Harvard University Press, 1958.

Brown, W. Norman. "Mythology of India," Section 2: "The Process of Creation," in *Mythologies of the Ancient World*, ed. Samuel

Noah Kramer. Anchor Books, Garden City, N.Y. : Doubleday & Co., 1961.

Brown, W. Norman, "The Creation Myth of the *Rig Veda.*" *Journal of the American Oriental Society* 62:85-98.

Brown, W. Norman. *The Mahimnastāva*. Poona, India: American Institute of Indian Studies, Publication No. 1. 1965.

Capra, Fritjof. *The Tao of Physics*. Paperback ed. Boulder, Colorado : Shambhala Publications, 1975.

Chatterji, Jagdish Chandra. *Kàshmir Śaivism*. (Śaivism spelled "Shaivaism" in the title.) Srinagar: Research & Publication Department, 1962.

Dasgupta, Surendranath. *A History of Indian Philosophy*. 5 vols. Cambridge: Cambridge University Press, 1963.

Dumont, P.E. "The Indic God Aja Ekapad, the One-Legged Goat," *Journal of the American Oriental Society*. 53:326-334.

Edgerton, Franklin, trans. *Vikrama's Adventures*, or the *Thirty-two Tales of the Throne*. Harvard Oriental Series, vols. 26-27. Cambridge: Harvard University Press, 1926. I. Translation, II, Text.

Eggeling, Julius, trans. *Śatapatha Brāhmaṇa According to the Text of the Madhyandina School. Sacred Books of the East*, vols. 12, 26, 41, 43, 44. London: Oxford University Press, 1900. Reprint; Delhi: Motilal Banarasidass, 1963.

Eliade, Mircea. *Yoga Immortality and Freedom*. 2d. ed., trans. Willard R. Trask. Bollingen Series LVI, Princeton University Press, 1969.

Gheraṇḍa Saṁhitā. Trans. Śrīś Chandra Vasu. 3d ed. London: Theosophical Publishing House, 1976.

Goetz, Hermann. *The Art of India*. 2d ed. New York: Greystone Press, 1964.

J. Gonda. Viṣṇuism and Śivaism: A Comparison. London: University Press, The Athlone Press, 1970.

J. Gonda. *Loka:* World and Heaven in the Veda. Amsterdam: N.V Noord-Hollandsche Uitgevers Maatschappiji, 1966.

Griffith, Ralph T.H., trans. *Hymns of the Rig-Veda*. 2 vols. Chowkhamba Sanskrit Studies. Vol. 35. Varanasi: Chowkhamba Sanskrit Series Office,1963.

Gupta, Sanjukta, trans. *Lakṣmī Tantra*: A Pancaratra Text. Leiden; E.J. Brill, 1972.

Haṭhayogapradīpikā of Svātmārāma, with Commentary of Brahmananda. Trans. Srinivasa Iyengar. Madras: The Theosophical Publishing House, 1972.

Heesterman, J.C. *The Ancient Indian Royal Consecration*: The Rājasūya Described According to the Yajus Texts and Annotated. The Hague; S-Gravenhage, Mouton & Co., 1957.

Hume, Robert Ernest, trans. *The Thirteen Principal Upanishads*. 2d rev. ed. London: Oxford University Press, 1931, 4th impression, 1958.

Kaviraj, Gopinath. *Aspects of Indian Thought*. Burdwan: The University of Burdwan, 1966.

Keith, Arthur Berriedale. *The Religion and Philosophy of the Veda and Upanishads*. Harvard Oriental Series, Vol. 32. Cambridge: Harvard University Press, 1925. Reprint. 2 vols. Delhi: Motilal Banarsidass, 1970.

Keith, Arthur Berriedale, trans. *The Veda of the Black Yajus School entitled Taittirīya Saṁhitā*. 2 vols. Harvard Oriental Series 18, 19. Cambridge; Harvard University Press, 1914. Reprint. Delhi: Motilal Banarasidass, 1967.

Kramrisch, Stella. *The Hindu Temple*. 2 vols. Calcutta, 1946. Reprint. 2 vols. Delhi: Motilal Banarasidass, 1980

Kramrisch, Stella. *The Art of India*. London, Phaidon Press, 1955.

Kuiper, F.B. J. "The Three Strides of Viṣṇu," in *Indological Studies in Honor of W. Norman Brown*, ed. Ernest Bender, American Oriental Society Series, Vol. 47. New Haven: American Oriental Society, 1962.

Lalitā-Sahāsranāman with Bhāskararāya's Commentary. Trans. R. Ananthakrishna Sastry. 2d. ed. Madras: The Theosophical Publishing House, 1951. Reprint, 1970.

Macdonell, Arthur Anthony, trans. *A Vedic Reader for Students*. London: Oxford University Press, 1917. 6th impression, 1965.

Macdonell, Arthur Anthony, and Keith, Arthur Berriedale, *Vedic Index of Names and Subjects*. 1st ed. 1912. 3d reprint. Delhi: Motilal Banarasidass, 1967.

Mahābhārata, trans. Pratap Chandra Roy. 12 vols. 2d ed. Bombay: Chetana Ltd., 1960.

Mahadevan, T.M.P. *Outlines of Hinduism*. 2d ed. Bombay: Chetana Ltd., 1960.

Mallman, Marie Thérèse de. *Les Enseignements Iconographiques de L'Agni-Purāṇa*. Paris: Presses Universitaires de France, 1963.

Natarajan, B, *The City of the Cosmic Dance*. New Delhi: Orient Longman Ltd., 1974.

Nikhilananda, Swami. *The Upanishads* Abridged ed. Harper Torchbooks. New York: Harper & Row, 1965.

Pal, Pratapaditya. *Vaiṣṇava Iconography in Nepal*. Calcutta, Asiatic Society, 1970.

Pillai, J.M. Somasundaram. *The University's Environs: Cultural and HIstorical*, A Silver Jubilee Souvenir of the Annamalai University. 4th impression, rev. and enl. Annamalainagar; Annamalai University, 1963.

Pott, P.H. *Yoga and Yantra*. Trans. Rodney Needham. The Hague; Martinus Nijhoff, 1966.

Przyluski, Jean, "Symbolism of the Sarnath Pillar," trans. Father Joseph van Troy, in V.S. Agrawala *Chakra-Dvaja, the Wheel-Flag of India*. Varanasi; Prithivi Prakashan, 1964.

Rao, T.A. Gopinatha. *Elements of Hindu Iconography*. 2d ed. Madras. 1914. Reprint. 2 vols. in 4 separate books. New York: Paragon Reprint Corp., Distributor: Delhi: Motilal Banarasidass, 1968.

Rowland, Benjamin. *The Art and Architecture of India*. Baltimore: Penguin Books, reprinted 1959.

Sagan, Carl. *Cosmos*. New York: Random House, 1980.

Śakta Upaniṣads, trans. A.G. Krishan Warrier. Madras: Adyar Lubrary and Research Center, 1967.

Schrader, F. Otto. *Introduction to the Pāñcarātra and the Ahirbudhnya Saṁhitā*. Madras: Adyar Library, 1916.

Shankaranarayan, S. *The Śrī Chakra*. 2d ed. Pondicherry: Dipti Publications, 1973.

Singh, Madanjeet. *Himalayan Art*. Unesco Art Books. New York: Macmillan, 1968. Collier Books ed. New york: Collier Books, 1971.

Sircar, D.C. *The Śakta Piṭhas*. Delhi: Motilal Banarasidass, 1948.

Sircar, D. C., ed. *The Śakti Cult and Tārā*. Calcutta: University of Calcutta, 1967.

Śiva Saṁhitā, trans. Rai Bahadur Srisa Chandra Vasu. 2d ed. New Delhi: Oriental Books Reprint Corporation, 1975.

Staal, Frits. *AGNI*: The Vedic Ritual of the Fire Altar, 2 vols. Berkeley: The Asian Humanities Press, 1983.

Tucci, Guiseppe. *The Theory and Practice of the Maṇḍala*, Trans. Alan Houghton Broderick. London: Rider & Co., 1961.

Van Buitenen, J.A.B. "Akṣara." *Journal of the American Oriental Society*, 69: 176-187.

Van Buitenen, J.A.B. "Vājapeya: English Commentary." A 13-page account of the entire ritual of the Vājapeya performed in Poona in the 1950's recorded on sound film.

Wayman, Alex, "The Human Body as Microcosm in India, Greek Cosmology and Sixteenth Century Europe." *History of Religions*, Vol. 2, Novemeber 1982.

Whitney, William Dwight, trans. *Atharva-Veda*. 2 vols. Harvard Oriental Series, vols. 7, 8. Cambridge: Harvard University Press, 1905. Reprint, Delhi: Motilal Banarasidass, 1962.

Wilson, J.H., trans. *Viṣṇu Purāṇa*. 3d ed. Calcutta: Punthi Pustak, 1961.

Woodroofe, Sir John (Avalon, Arthur), trans. *The Serpent Power*. 6th ed. Madras: Ganesh & Co. 1960.

Woodroffe, Sir John. *The Garland of Letters*. 4th ed. Madras: Ganesh & Co., 1963.

Woodroofe, Sir John (Avalon, Arthur). trans. *Principles of Tantra*, Madras: Ganesh & Co. 1960.

Woodroofe, Sir John (Avalon, Arthur). *Śakti and Śakta*. Madras: Ganesh & Co. 1959.

Woodroffe, Sir John. *The Tantrarāja Tantra*. Madras: Ganesh & co., 1954.

Woodroffe, Sir John (Avalon, Arthur), trans. *Hymn to Kālī*: Karpūrādi Stotra. 2nd. rev. ed. Madras: Ganesh & Co., 1953.

Woodroffe, Sir John (Avalon, Arthur), trans. *The Great Liberation: Mahānirvāṇa Tantra*. 4th ed. Madras: Ganesh & Co., 1963.

Zimmer, Heinrich. *The Art of Indian Asia*, ed. and completed by Joseph Campbell. 2 vols. New York: Pantheon Books, 1955.

INDEX